NO EXCUSE

The Commitment of Living
a Christ-Centered Life

Allen Robinson

NO EXCUSE
THE COMMITMENT OF LIVING A CHRIST-CENTERED LIFE

iUniverse books may be ordered through booksellers or by contacting:

iUniverse
1663 Liberty Drive
Bloomington, IN 47403
www.iuniverse.com
844-349-9409

ISBN: 978-1-6632-3614-2 (sc)
ISBN: 978-1-6632-3613-5 (e)

Print information available on the last page.

iUniverse rev. date: 02/22/2022

CONTENTS

INTRODUCTION

WHEN WE THINK ABOUT THE CHRISTIAN LIFE, WE MUST LOOK AT all the evidence the Word of God has given us and come to the conclusion that we must examine our hearts to see the call to live in obedience through the new covenant that we have been given through Jesus Christ. The evidence is crystal clear, we are called as followers of Christ, to be committed to living a life focused on him.

There is a practical importance of harmonizing one's walk with one's talk. If we are truly committed to living a life in Jesus Christ there has to be evidence from the testimony of a changed life because of him.

Throughout the book of James, we see a continual exhortation for followers of Christ to live a life of maturity and holiness; to take the abstract concept of faith and make it a firm foundation in our lives.

A faith-filled life requires us to address each area of our life that does not fit our Christian testimony and correct those areas to help experience the fullness of an active Christian life. If we don't put into practice everything that the Word of God gives us, our lives won't change.

What it all comes down to is our attitude. Our attitude is at the center of everything that we think, desire, say, and do. That's why having an eternal and God-focused attitude is imperative to help us live a committed life and really because of this we have no excuse if we are living by the power of the Holy Spirit.

1

THROUGH THE STORM

WITH ALMOST EVERY SPORT THERE IS SOMETHING CALLED A follow-through. The follow-through is a continuous flow of movement. For example, if you were to hit a ball with a bat, instead of stopping once you have made contact with a ball, you want to accelerate as hard as you can in your swing so that your maximum velocity is focused at the point of contact. Basically, you should never be slowing down when you make contact with the ball. If you are swinging properly, then you will naturally "follow through" with the action. The lack of a follow-through implies that you're not putting as much power on the ball as you could be. The same idea of the follow through with hitting a ball is the same follow through with the Christian life. We do not stop growing once we become saved, we must continue to grow daily in our relationship with God.

THE COMMITMENT OF LIVING
A CHRIST-CENTERED LIFE

What would happen if you became saved and your faith never grew? Your Christian faith would become stagnant. There would be no growth, no development, and no follow-through in living a Godly life.

Imagine your life was a pond. If the pond has a constant source of water flowing into it and out of it, it would be thriving with life. Now if your pond had no water flowing into it, it would become stagnant and lifeless. If you have ever smelled a stagnant pond, then you understand the difference between the two.

As Christians, we have been called to live a Christ-centered life. With Christ as the central focus in our life, we have a living water source, flowing into our lives through the Holy Spirit. Jesus said in John 7:37-38, "If anyone is thirsty, let him come to Me and drink. 38 The one who believes in Me, as the Scripture said, 'From his innermost being will flow rivers of living water.'"

This is an example of what our life should look like, a life overflowing with the fresh, new, living water of Christ in us. As a result of this living water, God's Word will flow from our life with an abundance of the truth. 2 Timothy 2:15 says, "Be diligent to present yourself approved to God as a workman who does not need to be ashamed, accurately handling the word of truth."

The idea of the word "approved" is the Greek word "doemoss", (Dok-E-Moss), which means "not counterfeit". As believers we are called to have a genuine testimony of Jesus Christ in our life, to live a Bona Fide Christian Life. This idea of the genuine Christian life is the same idea that James gives us when he says that we may be perfect, complete lacking nothing.

> James 1:2-4 "Consider it all joy, my brethren, when you encounter various trials, 3 knowing that the testing of your faith produces endurance. 4 And let endurance have its perfect result, so that you may be perfect and complete, lacking in nothing."

Have you ever bought a brand new item like a curling iron, a hairdryer, or a toaster? The first thing you do when you open the package is that you see the instructions followed by the warning. These manufacturers' warnings were put in to help keep you safe. These warnings may say, "Do not use the hairdryer in the shower." Why would they put these warnings on the products? Because at some time, someone has tried to use the product incorrectly and then tried to sue the company.

Now we are not like those who would do such a thing as incorrectly using a product, but are we living as God has instructed us on how we should live the Christian life? Do we act according to what God's Word says? As with all scripture, the Bible should change our lives the more we read it.

James begins by writing this one word, "when". It is "not if, not maybe, or by chance," but "when you encounter various trials". He opens his letter by illustrating how we should be thinking when we face those times of life that we do not expect. When we encounter the storms, trials, and troubles that we will have in our lives.

Let's get real here, the world does not see troubles as a reason to rejoice. How many of you got up this morning and said, "Praise the Lord I got a new pain?" How many of you got up this morning and thanked God for the problems of the day? None of us. When cancer and illness affect us, when fires and hurricanes come, when a divorce happens, this is the time we find ourselves questioning what God is doing in our life or why he allowed the problems to happen.

THE CHRISTIANS VIEWPOINT WHEN THE TRIALS COME

As Christians, we are to have a different viewpoint when the trials come in our life. We are told to rejoice, not in the problems of life, but that God is working through us, either to grow us, develop us, or to help encourage others who may be going through the same experiences we are going through. When those times happen in life our first response is never joy when the trials come, it is usually "why me".

Have you heard the saying, "What doesn't kill you makes you stronger"? How many of us believe that? God is not out to get you, God is not giving you trials because it's fun, He is doing something in you to achieve the goal for your life.

> Romans 8:28-30 "And we know that God causes all things to work together for good to those who love God, to those who are called according to His purpose. 29 For those whom He foreknew, He also predestined to become conformed to the image of His Son, so that He would be the firstborn among many brothers and sisters; 30 and these whom He predestined, He also called; and these whom He called, He also justified; and these whom He justified, He also glorified."

Let's take a moment to break this verse down together. "For those whom He foreknew, speaking of God knowing all things. "He also predestined", meaning God had a plan to bring us back into a relationship with God through the atonement of Jesus dying for our sins on the cross. "To become conformed to the image of His Son", how do we do this? By accepting Jesus as our Savior, by growing in our relationship with Jesus Christ, and by developing the characteristics of Christ in our life. God's purpose for our life is nothing less than Christlikeness. "So that He would be the firstborn among many brethren; and these whom He predestined, He also called; and these whom He called, He also justified; and these whom He justified, He also glorified." He planned it out, he carried it out, and he calls us out to be justified, sanctified and one day glorified through his glorious plan.

THE GOAL OF OUR LIFE

Why should we "Consider it all joy", when the trials in life come? Because we know, "That the testing of your faith produces endurance." What good is endurance?

When I went to the Criminal Justice Academy, one of our daily activities was running. I have to tell you, I don't like to run, I despise running. The instructors gave us one instruction, run. I started with a good pace, but after the first hundred yards, (really it was probably just twenty feet), I would lose my momentum, and then I would have to walk. Why? Because I had no endurance. I had not built up the strength to run a long distance. I was not prepared to go the distance of the run. James is saying the same thing to us as believers, it's going to be a marathon, not a sprint. When we are given the trials of this life, this is where we put our dependence on Jesus for his strength, for his Words, for his plan of growth. Not to just run, but what does James 1:4 say? James 1:4 "And let endurance have its perfect result, so that you may be perfect and complete, lacking in nothing."

God's goal in our life is to become perfected to the image of Jesus Christ. To let endurance, those things that come into our life, strengthen you in Jesus Christ, so that you may have perfect results. We, as believers, are in the process of being sanctified. What does it mean to be sanctified? Sanctification is the work of God's grace, renewing us to the image of God until we become perfected to the image of his Son. It is the process where we are enabled more and more to die unto sin and live unto righteousness. It is a continuing change by God in us, freeing us from sinful habits and forming in us Christlike affections, dispositions, and virtues.

What other part of life can you say, I have perfect results? Which one of us is perfect in anything? No one, because the results of our actions are imperfect because we are sinners. But yet, when Christ is at work in your life, he will always have perfect results. God has not given up on us, he constantly is working to mold us and shape us into the image of Christ.

> Jeremiah 18:5 "Then the word of the Lord came to me saying, 6 "Can I not, O house of Israel, deal with you as this potter does?" declares the Lord. "Behold, like the clay in the potter's hand, so are you in My hand, O house of Israel."

God is always at work in our life, making us, molding us, and perfecting us into who we are to be, and what we are to look like until we reach the perfect image of Jesus. God is developing us into mature men or women of faith and God will continue to work in us through the trials, through the pain, until we reach that point where he looks at us and sees his Son.

BECOMING PERFECTED TO THE IMAGE OF JESUS CHRIST

One day a young man approached the foreman of a logging crew and asked for a job. The foreman said, "Let's see you fell a tree first." The young man stepped forward and skillfully felled a large tree. The foreman was impressed and said to the young man, "You can start on Monday". The young man worked hard during the week, but by the end of the week, the foreman said to the young man, "We have no need for you anymore. You have fallen behind in your felling of the trees". The young man shouted, "How could that be? I have worked really hard. Please don't fire me". The foreman thought for a minute, how could this young man so skilled fall in his production of felling trees? Then the foreman asked, "Have you been sharpening your ax"? The young man replied, "No, I have been working too hard to take time for that"! (K. Hughes, Liberating Ministry From The Success Syndrome, Tyndale.)

Can the same thing be said about us as Christians? We are busy with the work of the Lord, yet we never take time to sharpen ourselves with the Word of God. To navigate through our lives, we need to have our tools sharp more than we need to have our lives busy.

> Ephesians 4:11-12 "And He gave some as apostles, and some as prophets, and some as evangelists, and some as pastors and teachers, 12 for the equipping of the saints for the work of service, to the building up of the body of Christ; 13 until we all attain to the unity of the faith, and of the knowledge of the Son of God, to a mature man, to the measure of the stature which belongs to the fullness of Christ.

The great news for us as believers is that God is still at work in you. God is developing our life through his Word and is in the process of bringing us to the point that we are unified in the faith that measures up to the fullness of his Son. God is working in your frailties, he is working in your pain, and he is working through you, even if you don't see it. Sometimes we need to take those moments in our lives to see how God is working in us. How is God using you in your circumstances? How is he reaching those around you? How is God shaping you?

We know that while we are still here on this earth, God is still working in our life. We can never really know for sure the depth of our character or the depth of our faith until it is tested.

> James 1:5-7 "But if any of you lacks wisdom, let him ask of God, who gives to all generously and without reproach, and it will be given to him. 6 But he must ask in faith without any doubting, for the one who doubts is like the surf of the sea, driven and tossed by the wind. 7 For that man ought not to expect that he will receive anything from the Lord, 8 being a double-minded man, unstable in all his ways."

OUR DEVELOPMENT INTO THE
MATURITY OF FAITH

We may not understand what God is doing, but we know whatever he is doing is perfect. God never said he was going to give you all the answers, but he did say if you desire wisdom ask for it. This may be where you find yourself today. You may not understand the reasons why, but we know that God does. He has a perfect plan for your life even in our uncertainty.

What good is the knowledge that we have if we do not use the wisdom of God for his purpose? What is the difference between wisdom and knowledge? Wisdom is the ability to discern or judge what is true, right, or lasting. Knowledge, on the other hand, is information gained through experience, learning, or reasoning.

Knowledge understands when the traffic light has turned red and wisdom applies the brakes. Knowledge sees the quicksand; wisdom walks around it. Knowledge memorizes the Word of God and wisdom obeys it. Knowledge learns about God, and wisdom loves Him.

Do we trust God in his direction for our life? I know that is a hard question to answer because we always want to know what comes next in our life. It is a controlling factor and we all have it.

We want to control everything that happens in our life because it gives us a comfort factor in how we live. Do you trust God? God is always sovereign; he ultimately controls all that happens in the world around us and in our lives.

We can ask ourselves; do we trust God or not? We cannot say, "I trust God today, but not tomorrow". Some say, "I can trust Him with my salvation, but when it comes to finances, I'm not sure God is big enough to handle them". Or "I know God created the Heavens and the earth, but I think this problem in my life is way too big for God". No matter what circumstance we may find ourselves in, do you believe God is big enough and strong enough to handle any problems in your life? One determination for your answer is if you believe God is in control then why do you worry?

At some time in our life, we have all faced storms that come up on a usual basis. On the east coast, it is usually during June through November that we face hurricane season.

If you remember in 2005, Hurricane Katrina had slammed into New Orleans and the Mississippi Gulf Coast and caused severe devastation to all the surrounding areas in the south. In Luke chapter 8, we see a storm that came upon experienced fishermen and bought them to their knees.

> Luke 8:22-23 "One day Jesus said to his disciples,
> "Let us go over to the other side of the lake." So
> they got into a boat and set out. 23 As they sailed,
> he fell asleep. A squall came down on the lake, so
> that the boat was being swamped, and they were
> in great danger."

It's probably been a busy day of ministry for Jesus and His disciples when He tells them to follow Him to the lake known as the Sea of Galilee. They are going to the other side of the sea, which is about six to seven miles across. It hadn't been long before Jesus goes to the front of the boat and falls asleep.

If you have ever seen the Sea of Galilee or been there on a tour you would notice that the water's surface is about 680 feet below sea level. All around the sea, it is surrounded by steep hills and mountains on every side. When the cool air comes sweeping through those hills, and suddenly encounters the warm air that's been trapped over the water, it can create some vicious storms.

Normally, on a calm day, it would have taken about six hours to cross the sea, but in this storm, it would have seemed like forever. As Jesus and his disciples are partway across the sea, it happened that one of those unexpected storms falls upon them. You would have thought that these men would have been prepared for an encounter with such a storm, being experienced fishermen, but on this day, it was going to test the disciples in every way possible.

Imagine with me, as the sky has gotten dark, and the wind begins to blow. The vicious wind hurls the raindrops, like icy darts pelting down on you with stinging pain, the waves begin to swell past the edges of the boat, and it begins to fill with water, and although you are all bailing as fast as you can, you can't keep ahead. The storm winds are so strong the sail does nothing to help the disciples. You are soaked through to the skin. You look down, and when the lightning flashes you see that the water is mid-way up your calves. You may have been on the sea before in a storm, but not like this. With all they had tried to do they are at the point that they believe you are going to die – and this is not an idle fear, you've seen death, you've seen danger, you've been in difficult situations before but never like this. You know, "we're going to drown!".

Imagine the waves of fear these men must be feeling. Working as hard as they can and trying anything, to no avail, fighting the storm with whatever strength they have, and the water keeps rising in the boat. Can you imagine how the disciples felt that day? Verse 23 says, "...A squall came down on the lake, so that the boat was being swamped, and they were in great danger." In Matthew 8:24, it says that "the waves swept over the boat." This was one serious storm. They had a crisis on their hands.

There are modern storms that we deal with, and I think we have all had those moments where we feel unprepared for the storms we face. Maybe even at this moment, you feel like life is crashing in. You feel battered, weighed down, exhausted, and overwhelmed, with no end and no hope in sight.

Someone may be feeling an economic or financial crisis. Maybe it is an emotional crisis, possibly a relational crisis, or even a spiritual crisis. It seems as if life is raging, and we are being attacked on all sides and we feel like we are going to drown. Have you ever felt like Jesus isn't there?

What do we usually do when the storms come in life? We try to work it out according to our way. We do our best to fix things the best way we know-how and find that we are just chasing the wind. Why did it take so long for the disciples to come to get Jesus, or even a better question, why did they even fear with Jesus in the boat?

In the verses ahead the disciples finally turn to Jesus. How long has the storm been raging? Long enough. They probably thought they could handle it on their own. They thought their skill and experience were enough to ride it out without ever bothering Jesus, but only when it gets really bad do they turn to Jesus and wake Him up. I wondered if it had been me, would I have gone back and sat next to Jesus? What was the disciple's final answer to hope? Jesus!

> Luke 8:24 "They came up to Jesus and woke Him,
> saying, "Master, Master, we are perishing!" And
> He got up and rebuked the wind and the surging
> waves, and they stopped, and it became calm."

I can imagine they finally came to their senses and asked themselves, "what are we doing, lets wake Jesus, He can fix this for us, He can save us!"

Did Jesus know the storm was coming? Absolutely. Then why did Jesus allow them to go into the storm? To teach them. Remember the disciples were seeing all the miracles of Jesus, but they had not yet faced the situation themselves where they needed Jesus.

As Jesus was woken, he immediately rebuked the wind and the raging waves. Suddenly the storm stopped, and all was calm. In an instant, everything stops. At this point, the disciples had to ask themselves who Jesus truly is.

> Luke 8:25b "But they were fearful and amazed,
> saying to one another, "Who then is this, that
> He commands even the winds and the water, and
> they obey Him?"

This miracle forced the disciples deeper in their experience of who Jesus is, leading them still closer to see that Jesus is the Son of God and not just a powerful teacher or prophet like Elijah.

Jesus asks them a simple, yet complex question, "Where is your faith?" To answer the question, "Who is Jesus?", the answer must come from the question Jesus asked in Luke 8:25a "And He said to them, "Where is your faith?" What is needed more than

13

anything else in getting through our storms is having a deep-rooted faith in Christ. Everyone has faith in something. The issue for believers is: what do you place your faith in? We can place our faith in our physical senses, touch, taste, smell, hearing, and sight. We can place our faith in our emotions, or we can place our faith in the God who created us and in his inspired divine word. This, of course, was the issue with the disciples. Hebrews 11:1 says, "Now faith is the certainty of things hoped for, a proof of things not seen". If it can be verified, we don't need faith. Faith is for that which lies beyond our ability to reason.

> Hebrews 11:6 "And without faith, it is impossible to please Him, for the one who comes to God must believe that He exists and that He proves to be One who rewards those who seek Him."

The same can be said for us when the trails come into our life. Are we focusing on the trials that are occurring or on what God is doing in us to perfect us and to build us up in the faith? Sure, it's easy to have faith when life is going well, but do we focus on God during difficult times or when we are put into uncomfortable situations? If faith is not built in the routines of life, it's not strong in the storms. Faith is built upon what we can trust. Faith is built upon that which is foundational, and both are built upon Jesus Christ for believers.

As Jesus calms the storm, the disciples responded, by asking the question, "who is this? He commands even the winds and the water, and they obey him." (Luke 8:25)

Haven't the disciples seen his power? Have they not seen the miracles? Did they understand who Jesus is? Jesus is the one who is with us in our storms and trials of life, he is the one who enables us to face the tragedies and suffering with the assurance that he is with us, and he will carry us through, no matter what.

When you are facing a storm or a trial in your life, there is no more important equipment than having the Word of God. Whatever the storm, there is no greater help to have than the one who has authority over every storm. Whatever storm you may be facing, know that God will be with you. That is why the Psalmist could say, "God is our refuge and strength, an ever-present help in trouble" (Psalm 46:1).

If we are going to grow our faith, we must grow through God's working in our lives and seek His help. The disciples did not fully understand who Jesus really was, and sometimes we don't either. We have storms that come into our lives, and we ask the same thing that did the disciple asked; 'Lord, don't you care?' And Jesus responded by saying, 'Don't you have any faith?'

I think we need to take our walk with Jesus very seriously. We need to expect extraordinary events out of ordinary circumstances.

> James 1:2-4 "Consider it pure joy, my brothers and sisters, whenever you face trials of many kinds, 3 because you know that the testing of your faith produces perseverance. 4 Let perseverance finish its work so that you may be mature and complete, not lacking anything."

Amazingly, so many people deal with the worries and anxieties of life. Believe it or not, Christians also have this fear of what comes next, what burden must I bear, and what unforeseen circumstance is about to come into my life?

Are you willing to grow in God? Are you willing to go through the burdens so that you may become closer to him? Sometimes our trials come because of what we are doing. This includes the sin in our life, the reactions to the choices that we make that are against how God has called us to live.

> Galatians 6:7-8 "Do not be deceived, God is not mocked; for whatever a person sows, this he will also reap. 8 For the one who sows to his own flesh will reap destruction from the flesh, but the one who sows to the Spirit will reap eternal life from the Spirit."

Are you dragging your feet when God has called you to go? Are you staying quiet when God has called you to speak? Are you not doing as God directs? God is not punishing you for not doing something, but he is working in you so that, "You may be perfect and complete, lacking in nothing." Here is the question we need to ask, what are you seeking? Is it a relief from the burdens you bear? Is it the glory of the riches of this world? Is it your desire for the growth and maturity in Christ Jesus and are you truly seeking God's kingdom first?

In your struggles and trials, do you believe that God is in control? Have you done as Proverbs 3:5-6 say, "Trust in the LORD with all your heart and do not lean on your own understanding. 6In all your ways acknowledge Him, And He will make your paths straight."

Believers have the joy of knowing that God is at work in their life, through their struggles, their growth and their development. Yes, there may be unpleasant times, but as we said before God

Knows what He is doing. God is working his perfect will in your life to get the perfect results that only he can achieve. Philippians 2:13 "for it is God who is at work in you, both to will and to work for His good pleasure."

Do you know what the storms of life do for us? They reveal where we've been placing our faith.

2

HAVING THE PROPER PERSPECTIVE

THE DOG ATE MY HOMEWORK, THERE WAS TRAFFIC ON THE WAY to work, my alarm didn't go off, and the devil made me do it. These are just a few excuses that at some point in our life we may have used. We can have an excuse for anything.

In our lives, we have all come to use an excuse now or then. What are the reasons we use excuses? Most of the time it is to get us out of trouble or to keep from being punished.

Do you remember the times when you thought you were in trouble? If I heard my mother use my full name, I knew I was in trouble. I would automatically start thinking, "what did I do?" How often do we use excuses to try and escape the blame for what we did? For me, it was my sister's fault, or the dog's fault, anyone else, but me.

This is nothing new. Excuses have been around since the beginning of creation in the Garden of Eden. Look at Adam and Eve in Genesis. God gave only one command, Genesis 2:17 "Do not eat from the tree of the knowledge of good and evil you shall not eat, for in the day that you eat from it you will surely die."

It's simple right? One command. God said everything else is open to you. What happened? They both ate from the fruit of the tree of the knowledge of good and evil. Both Adam and

Eve had eaten the fruit and were confronted by God. When God confronted Adam, Adam turned to God and said in Genesis 3:12; "The woman whom you gave to be with me, she gave me from the tree, and I ate." Adam was saying, "It's your fault, God. That woman you put here led me astray"! Then God turned to Eve and Eve said, "The serpent deceived me, and I ate." He is the one to blame.

WE ONLY HAVE OUR SELF TO BLAME

When it comes to sin, isn't that what each one of us tries to do, blame someone else for the sin?

Think about it, it's the parent's fault for not raising their children right, it's the government's fault for taking prayer and Bible out of schools, it's the judge's fault for taking down the ten commandments, it is the website's fault for having the filth on the internet, it the casino's fault for having gambling. The list goes on and on. How about this one which many people like to use, "It's the Devil's fault, he is the one that made me do it"?

When it comes to sin in our life, we have only ourselves to blame. At what point do we ever look to ourselves? At what point do we ever accept the blame? Most people would like to blame God for all the problems of this world, including the sin and struggles we go through.

First, understand this, God is not going to make you do anything, we have free will. A choice to either obey or disobey.

1 Corinthians 10:13 "No temptation has overtaken you but such as is common to man; and God is faithful, who will not allow you to be tempted beyond what you are able, but with the temptation will provide the way of escape also, so that you will be able to endure it."

Addressing the Problem in Our Life

God has given us the Holy Spirit, because we have believed that salvation comes only through Jesus Christ and our relationship with him, to guide us, to help us, to lead us, but we like to sin. We often desire sin. The problem that we have is that the Holy Spirit is always speaking, but we just aren't listening. Our free will gives us the choice to either sin or to run away, listen to God or to disobey, to be faithful to his word, or to disregard it.

So why do we sin? How does sin overtake us? James 1:14 says, "But each one is tempted when he is carried away and enticed by his own lust." What happens is that we tell ourselves, "I can't stop it, I can't fix it, I can't help it and the list goes on and on. Instead of making excuses, what we should be doing is addressing the problem of the sin in our lives and we should be addressing the spiritual cause of the problem in our life.

Where does sin start? In your heart, in your will, and your mind. No one forces us to sin, we do it willingly. You may say, "How can you say that?" Think about it, who caused you to think about the wrong things? You did. Who thought about carrying the action of sin out? You did. Who put the sin into action? You did!

When sin begins, it starts as a thought, it begins in your mind. Here is what many Christians get tripped up on, can Satan make you sin? No, but he can sure put things in your path to get your attention to tempt you. Maybe it is something you see or something you hear; sin always begins in the mind.

Did you ever have something from your past like hurt or something that had been done to you that caused you to get angry? It came into your mind and you started to think about that event and you got angry, why? Because we like to dwell in the past, in the hurts, and the sufferings.

The truth about who we are is that we are sinful people, with a sinful nature. Jeremiah 17:9 "The heart is more deceitful than all else and is desperately sick; who can understand it?" Even as Christians just because we accept the gift of salvation, that does not take away the sinful desires of our hearts.

When the Bible talks about our heart, it is referring to our will and our mind, they are the parts of us no one else sees. Sure, doctors can see your brain, your body, and the integrated details of your body, but they can never see your mind.

The problem of sin begins in our thinking, which is why God says the problem is in the heart and the mind. God starts at the root of our problem. Just like a vine that grows along a tree or a house, unless you dig up the root, the vine will always continue to grow.

> 2 Corinthians 10:5 "We are destroying specu-
> lations and every lofty thing raised up against
> the knowledge of God, and we are taking every
> thought captive to the obedience of Christ,"

The problem is not just in the sin or habit of sin, it is our mind. We cannot defeat sin unless we fix our minds.

> Ephesians 6:10-12 "Finally, be strong in the Lord and in the strength of His might. 11 Put on the full armor of God, so that you will be able to stand firm against the schemes of the devil. 12 For our struggle is not against flesh and blood, but against the rulers, against the powers, against the world forces of this darkness, against the spiritual forces of wickedness in the heavenly places."

The solution to defeating sin is first addressing the problem. If you have brain cancer, taking two aspirin and lying down is not going to fix the problem. If you have skin cancer, rubbing lotion on the skin will not fix the problem.

You cannot fight the sin if you allow the sin to control your mind. So, what do you do? You can't blame God; God is not the problem.

James 1:13 says, "Let no one say when he is tempted, "I am being tempted by God"; for God cannot be tempted by evil, and He does not tempt anyone."

You can't blame Satan. He can put the temptation out there but he can't make you sin. So, who is to blame? We are. But aren't we supposed to be Christians? Don't we have the Holy Spirit living in us? Yes, as Christians, we have the indwelling Holy Spirit to help us overcome sin, but we also have the choice to make because of our free will. If we sin, we have no excuse, we cannot blame the devil, we cannot blame our circumstances, we can only blame ourselves. Until we recognize that the problem resides within us, we will never solve the problem. Paul even speaks to his struggle with his sinful nature in Romans 7.

> Romans 7:17-18 "So now, no longer am I the one doing it, but sin which dwells in me. 18 For I know that nothing good dwells in me, that is, in my flesh; for the willing is present in me, but the doing of the good is not. 19 For the good that I want, I do not do, but I practice the very evil that I do not want. 20 But if I am doing the very thing I do not want, I am no longer the one doing it, but sin which dwells in me."

> James 1:16-17 "Do not be deceived, my beloved brethren. 17 Every good thing given and every perfect gift is from above, coming down from the Father of lights, with whom there is no variation or shifting shadow."

God is not here to make your life miserable, it's even blasphemy to suppose that God either tempts or makes us sin. Man has his own capacity for evil. For example, no parent has ever had to teach their children to sin. It comes naturally because of our sinful nature. We screamed to get our way. We threw temper tantrums, we cried and complained.

DO NOT LET SIN HAVE A PLACE IN YOUR MIND

We live in a fallen world that aligns with our old nature which says, "live for yourself" and "pleases yourself".

If you have been fishing, what do you use to attract the fish?

Bait. Baiting is what you do to lure unsuspecting animals out into the open from a position of safety to a place where they can be caught. Hunters sometimes use something called bait stations to attract animals. They come to the place where the bait station is because the food is a desire for them, and it is readily available. So is the same for us as believers. Satan makes the temptation of sin desirable. The more we think about that desire, the more we rationalize a way to achieve it. That's how sin works.

Paul tells us, in Galatians 5:16-17 "But I say, walk by the Spirit, and you will not carry out the desire of the flesh. 17 For the desire of the flesh is against the Spirit, and the Spirit against the flesh; for these are in opposition to one another, in order to keep you from doing whatever you want."

Overcoming Sin

How do we defeat sin? First, we need to acknowledge that there is sin in our life. Next is to change our thought process. Instead of dwelling on the sin, we need to remember how we are called to live as believers, by trusting God's promise that Jesus is better than anything sin gives us. Then we must not make any plans that open the door for sin's entry. "Make no provision for the flesh, to gratify its desires" (Romans 13:14). And lastly, we need to develop mental habits that continually renew the mind in God-centeredness (Romans 12:2; 2 Corinthians 4:16), that fixes attention daily on "the things of the Spirit" (Romans 8:5) and letting our minds dwell on whatever is true, honorable, just, pure, lovely, gracious, excellent, and worthy of praise (Philippians 4:8).

As believers in Jesus Christ, we now have real freedom not to sin. We can choose life and not death. We can trust Christ and resist the devil and we can put death to sin and pursue righteousness.

Remember that in the process of God working in us He sanctifies us. Sanctification consists of two elements: mortification and conformation. Mortification means we put sin to death. Conformation means we are being conformed to the image of Jesus Christ. Sanctification is not optional for a Christian; it is a requirement. Again, sanctification is the act of making or declaring something holy. This is what Jesus Christ is doing in our life daily.

The whole reason Jesus came was to bring the solution to our problem. Jesus came to give his life that we might be able to have a relationship with the Father again. He came to break us free from the bonds of slavery and to bring us hope. What is God calling for in our lives? Why does He give us a way out of temptation? Why has he given us his Son as our Savior? So that we might know him and understand his great love for us. We are no longer slaves of sin; we have been set free. Therefore, walk in freedom. We have the freedom to live a holy life.

> Romans 6:1-4 "What shall we say then? Are we to continue in sin so that grace may increase? 2 Far from it! How shall we who died to sin still live in it? 3 Or do you not know that all of us who have been baptized into Christ Jesus have been baptized into His death? 4 Therefore we have been buried with Him through baptism into death, so that, just as Christ was raised from the dead through the glory of the Father, so we too may walk in newness of life."

3

LISTEN, SPEAK AND ACT

WHEN I WAS YOUNGER, I USED TO BE A REVOLUTIONARY WAR reenactor and I had the privilege of working on the cannon crew. Being on the cannon crew one thing I learned was to anticipate the "bang". Once the fuse touched the powder it was bound to go off.

When working around loud noises most people use some kind of hearing protection. The hearing protection lowers the decibels of the noise and softens it to an acceptable level of hearing. Doctors have created something called a hearing aid for those who have trouble hearing. The television creators have created a device that completely takes away the hearing of most men called a remote control. How well do you hear God? Is the Holy Spirit's voice muffled because of your hearing or do you intently listen for God's voice?

When you take a hearing test the doctors will put you in a sound booth which will eliminate the ambient noise around you. They use a set of tones to test your hearing scale to see how productive your hearing is. I have something called tinnitus. Tinnitus is a constant ringing or sound in my ears which, when it becomes quiet, all I hear is the constant ringing. When taking a hearing test my doctors know when they reach the tone of my tinnitus, because I stop raising my hand during the test. I sit there waiting for the next tone.

BEING AN EFFECTIVE LISTENER

How many of us have gotten to the point in our life when we stop hearing God speak? Maybe because we are too busy or maybe it's because we are so preoccupied with everything else, we have become tone-deaf to his words.

Our society has been affected by the "Hurry up sickness" which hinders the important character trait of being quick to listen. You hear these excuses to justify not listening: "I'm too busy", "I have to run the kids everywhere they want to go", "I'm in a rush maybe later", "I have to work 70 hours a week to pay for all my stuff", "I'm exhausted I cannot listen!" "I don't have the time right now. I have things to do and people to see". Even after "I'm too tired, I worked 12 hours today", "Not now".

One of the most important key factors to any relationship is communication. Communication is not only sending messages but receiving them. It is a two-way form of listening and hearing and then speaking back to the one who is talking, basic communication. Communication usually breaks down if one or both partners fails to listen. You may be the person who is quick to speak and slow to listen, which has gotten many people in trouble that way.

Imagine communication is like tennis, two people hitting the ball back and forth over a net. What good would it be if one person just kept hitting the ball and the other person never returned it? You just stood there and watched the ball go around you. You would just quit because it would be no motivation for hitting a ball over a net. What if after you hit the ball over the net the other person would get angry and hit the ball as hard as they could aiming at your face? This also would cause you to stop playing. Communication involves both hearing and responding.

NOT ONLY HEARING BUT LISTENING

How important is it that we hear people correctly? Not only hearing but listening? Just because we can hear someone talking, that doesn't necessarily mean we are listening to what is being said. Sad to say this happens in our life all the time, not only in our relationships here on earth but also with our heavenly Father.

When it comes to hearing God, how often is it that we hear the leading of the Holy Spirit in our lives and yet, never listen to or act out to what he says? Or is it that we are not even hearing the Holy Spirit in our lives?

Our society is filled with a constant barrage of noise, music, announcements, advertisements, and games that seem to overwhelm us. When was the last time you sat quietly and did nothing, listened to nothing, worked on nothing, did not talk, had no music playing in your life? It is an empty sound.

If I were to ask you to say nothing for one minute, would there be an empty awkward silence? We would want to fill that emptiness with something, a cough, a sniffle, a clearing of the throat, closing of a book, or the shuffling of our feet. We tend to need to have some sort of noise to occupy the silence. What about the times when God says, "Be Still?"

I believe that the reason most people cannot distinguish between God's voice and other voices around them is that they have not spent time listening to God when he speaks. John 10:27 says, "My sheep hear My voice, and I know them, and they follow Me;"

When my uncle used to take me hunting, he would walk off in the distance and look for squirrels, so he told me. At one point when he was far enough away, he would put out a call to have me come and find him. It was a distinct call. Because he had put such a great distance between us, I had to listen very carefully to find which direction the sounds were coming from. At first, it was way off in the distance, then gradually as I got closer, it would become more defined that I was heading in the right direction.

He only made the call every 20-30 seconds. So, for a brief time, I would have to stop and listen carefully to which direction I heard the call. The closer I got to him the more defined his call was to me. We were both wearing camouflage. I couldn't see him, but I knew he was close because I would hear his call. Finally, I would see him and know that that was the place where I was to be. I was able to find him because I followed his call. When it comes to God in our lives, how well do you hear God's call? How well do we hear his instruction? How well are we at listening to God's direction in our life through the Holy Spirit? To be an effective listener we need to pay attention to his call, do what he says, in the way that he leads.

Silence and stillness have an essential place in our daily prayer life. There are many places in Scripture in which God directs the individual to silence and stillness. When we wait for God to speak to us in prayer it means we are listening attentively for what God wishes to convey to us. If one is sincere and if one wants to know what his will is, all one has to do is be quiet and wait for God to speak. I think Job said it best in Job 6:24 "Teach me, and I will be silent; and show me how I have done wrong."

BEING EFFECTIVE WITH OUR SPEECH

All of us have learned from an early age to listen. It is the first part of developing our speech. You may have remembered teaching your child to speak by constantly repeating the same words, like ma-ma or da-da, until your child learned the word and associated it with the item or person that related to the word or words.

It is the first part of communication. As a baby, if you are hungry you cry, if you are tired you cry, if you are upset you cry if you don't get your way you cried. It's funny that some of us handle things the same way as adults, it seems it is communication we never forget.

The second part of listening is knowing when to speak. Even in our early elementary years of school, we had to learn the process of learning when to speak and when it was our time to communicate. But how do we speak? Is it filled with edification and encouragement or hurt and tearing others down? Is it uplifting to God or destruction of his testimony in your life?

For me, I used to be a person who was quick to answer. I used to be quick-witted, but that came with a downfall in my life due to some words which I did not mean to say or the hurt that came when I opened my mouth. There is an art of knowing when to speak.

THE POWER OF WORDS

It is the Word preached that when heard, will lead to repentance and salvation. Romans 10:17 "So faith comes from hearing, and hearing by the Word of Christ." It is this Word that just by its very reading can move hearts and change minds (1 Timothy 4:13).

Language and communication are God's inventions, and, as such, Satan has a great interest in perverting them. Why else would God tell us to be "slow to speak and slow to anger?" When do our words hurt most? In the time of anger.

As we learned in the previous chapter, we are wicked people with wicked hearts. Jeremiah 17:9 "The heart is more deceitful than all else and is desperately sick; who can understand it?" The King James Bible says it in this way, "The heart is deceitful above all things, and desperately wicked: who can know it?"

This is what Satan does, he takes the good things of God that can be used for edification, grace, enlightenment, and love and makes them into something vulgar, dehumanizing, and certainly not pointed to the glory of God. Even as Christians, we need to recognize that there are jokes that we shouldn't laugh at, there is gossip that we should not participate in, and there are words that we shouldn't use. Our sanctified living is by the power of the Holy Spirit who is controlling the words we speak and focusing on saying only that which is useful for the edification and God-honoring purposes. Ephesians 4:29 says, "Let no unwholesome word proceed from your mouth, but only such a word as is good for edification according to the need of the moment so that it will give grace to those who hear."

Believe it or not, I have heard some professing Christians argue that using some degree of foul language is purposeful to convey certain truths or feelings.

This is a wrong statement. The problem is how can those who are unsaved see Jesus in you if they can't get past you?

Our words betray our hearts by revealing who we are and what we think. Some people can control their tongues better than others, but unless their hearts are right, eventually evil speaking will pour forth from their mouths. This is why we need to objectively evaluate our walks with Christ by taking a look at what we laugh at, what we say, and whether our words are abusive to others or offensive to God in any way.

> James 1:19-21 "This you know, my beloved brethren. But everyone must be quick to hear, slow to speak and slow to anger; 20 for the anger of man does not achieve the righteousness of God. 21 Therefore, putting aside all filthiness and all that remains of wickedness, in humility receive the word implanted, which is able to save your souls."

Anger is not something God wants us to be known for. It says in Proverbs 15:18 "A hot-tempered man stirs up strife, but the slow to anger calms a dispute." What does the average uncontrolled angry person do? They usually say things they shouldn't say. They insult people, they curse, they break things, they hurt themselves or they hurt others. Ephesians 4:31 says "Let all bitterness and wrath and anger and clamor and slander be put away from you, along with all malice." We are Christians. We are not supposed to act like the world, we have a higher standard of living because we have the Holy Spirit inside of us.

Now when the Bible says to be slow to anger, it is not talking here about getting a little upset. It is not talking about us getting annoyed with people. That happens all the time. What is your attitude when this happens? Do you let this situation get you so angry, that you get so upset it affects your testimony? The Bible is talking about anger where you have lost control.

HAVING A RIGHTEOUS ANGER

What does the Bible say about our anger? Is anger a sin? No. You can be angry over something that has happened, yet the Bible calls us to be angry, but don't sin. Ephesians 4:26-27 "Be angry, and yet do not sin; do not let the sun go down on your anger, 27 and do not give the devil an opportunity."

James hits the nail on the head when he tells us to be slow to anger. Why? Because unrighteous anger does not produce the type of Christian life God desires. Proverbs 14:17 "A quick-tempered man acts foolishly, and a man of evil devices is hated." "A quick-tempered man does foolish things!" As Christ-followers, we're appropriate to get upset over sin. Evils such as abuse, racism, pornography, and child sex trafficking should make us angry, but no matter how reprehensible the people or activities we're condemning, we still aren't justified to sin in our responses: Ephesians 4:26 "Be angry, and yet do not sin; do not let the sun go down on your anger". Those of us with confrontational personalities might want to ask yourself this question: Is my motive to be right or to be righteous before ripping into the offending parties?

The first mark of righteous anger is that it reacts against actual sin. It arises from an accurate perception of what is evil not in response to a violation of my preferences.

Paul understood that we are not responsible for being angry, because we all get angry, but we are responsible for how we respond to a situation when we are angry. Most people will say, "Well I expected to be angry. It just proves you're human." So, when we get angry and hit something, or hurt someone with our words, is that okay? The truth is they are wrong. Being angry in the wrong way doesn't prove you're human, it proves you are a sinner.

When people lose their temper, it can lead to sin. Not because you lost your temper, but because of your actions after you lost your temper. People cannot make excuses for bad behavior and we shouldn't either. Let's call it what it is, sin.

How many of you make excuses for things like anger and worry? How many of us make excuses for the sins in our life? Do you know how some people know how to push your buttons so you get angry with them easier than others? Why is it we have more patience with certain people and not others? It may be your husband or wife who can push your buttons, maybe your boss, or maybe the neighbor next door to you. Why do we let it get to us? For us as Christians, remember, 1 John 4:4 "greater is He who is in you than he who is in the world."

Unrighteous Anger Does Not Produce Godly Results

Many of us today need to take a good look at our lives and see if we are angry people.

> Luke 6:45 "The good man out of the good treasure of his heart brings forth what is good; and the evil man out of the evil treasure brings forth what is evil; for his mouth speaks from that which fills his heart."

Why do we become angry most of the time? We become angry because something has blocked our goal of what we were determined to do. People may say, "Well, didn't Jesus get angry when He turned the tables over at the temple?" Jesus in Matthew 21:13 was angry with what the spiritual leadership had done to the temple's worship. They made it into a den of thieves not a house of prayer. But note Jesus' anger is justified: Jesus was angry for others being blocked out of worship with God. People were coming between man and God and he saw his name being used to steal money from the poor. Jesus stood up for the ones who could not stand up for themselves. He was defending his sheep from the wolves. Can we be angry with those who have no voice in this world? Yes, but everything must be done decently and in order in a way that pleases God, that uplifts Jesus Christ. Not rioting, not destroying, and not holding grudges.

Do you remember when God had called Jonah to go to Nineveh to preach the salvation of God? What was Jonah's attitude? They could all die for he I cared. At the end of the book of Jonah as he sat under the vine waiting for the destruction of Nineveh.

> Jonah 4:5-9 "Jonah finally and reluctantly went
> and did what God asked. Then Jonah went east
> of the city and sat awaiting the destruction of
> God on Nineveh. Where Jonah was sitting God
> appointed a plant and it grew up over Jonah to
> be a shade over his head to deliver him from
> his discomfort. And Jonah was extremely happy
> about the plant. 7But God appointed a worm
> when dawn came the next day and it attacked

the plant and it withered. 8When the sun came up God appointed a scorching east wind, and the sun beat down on Jonah's head so that he became faint and begged with all his soul to die, saying, "Death is better to me than life." 9Then God said to Jonah, "Do you have good reason to be angry about the plant?" And he said, "I have good reason to be angry, even to death."

How did Jonah handle his anger? Was it justified? Could he have stayed in Nineveh and helped the people come to know God? Could he have not stayed and proclaimed more of God and his love for the people? The answer to both questions is yes. But Jonah held onto the anger inside and wished death upon the people of Nineveh. This was not righteous anger; it was hateful anger. The wrong anger does not produce the life of righteousness that God requires.

The meaning of this passage is not that our wrath will make God either more or less righteous; but that its tendency is not to produce that upright course of life, and love of truth, which God requires. This is not only with people outside our church but inside our church, inside our families, inside our own life. The next time you get angry, stop. Be slow to speak, and quick to hear. Hear God's direction in your life. It is always hard to hear God when pride gets in the way. Ephesians 4:26 "Be angry, and yet do not sin; do not let the sun go down on your anger, 27and do not give the devil an opportunity."

Remember who we represent as Christians. We are to model a Christ-like attitude in all that we do and say. How does the message of your life relay Jesus Christ to this world?

4

MODEL THE MESSAGE

"YOU CALL ME MASTER AND OBEY ME NOT, YOU CALL ME LIGHT and see me not, you call me the way and follow me not, you call me Life and desire me not. You call me wise and acknowledge me not, you call me fair and love me not, you call me rich and ask me not, and you call me eternal and seek me not. You call me gracious and trust me not, you call me noble and serve me not, you call me mighty and honor me not, and you call me just and fear me not. If I condemn you, blame me not." (Unknown author)

When you were younger do you remember putting together model airplanes? You would open the box and all of the pieces and parts of the airplane would be laid out in sections connected to the plastic tabs. The kit came with the glue, the decals, and instructions on how to put the plan together piece by piece. The goal of the project was to take all of the pieces and make the image of the plane that was on the front cover of the box.

How can we become the model for the message of Jesus Christ? It is amazing how you see the talents of so many people doing extraordinary things. It should not be a surprise to us that the more we do something, the better at it we become. They say "practice makes perfect" but I would like to interject, and say that "perfect practice makes perfect". How can we, as believers, perfect ourselves in Jesus Christ? How are the pieces of our life put together to find ourselves as the image on the box? To find ourselves matching the image of Jesus Christ from the Word of God?

PUTTING AWAY THE SIN IN OUR LIFE

Just like putting a model plane together, you needed to follow the instructions to complete the work to have your model plane match the picture on the box. The same can be said for our life as we are being perfected, fit together to match the image of Jesus Christ.

There are two parts to be perfected in Jesus Christ. The first part is taking something off, our old self, and the other is putting something on, the new life in Jesus Christ.

> Ephesians 4:21-24 "if indeed you have heard Him and have been taught in Him, just as truth is in Jesus, 22that, in reference to your former way of life, you are to rid yourselves of the old self, which is being corrupted in accordance with the lusts of deceit, 23and that you are to be renewed in the spirit of your minds, 24and to put on the new self, which in the likeness of God has been created in righteousness and holiness of the truth."

God knows us so well. Even in our poor views of ourselves, God gives us His view of how we live by putting off or putting aside "all filthiness and all that remains of wickedness".

Now if we are to take a good look at ourselves, we see that we have a heart of sin. It is our sinful nature. Does that give us an excuse to sin? No, of course not. The only thing that makes us different as believers are that we have accepted the gift of salvation and have been changed by Jesus Christ or at least we should be. Now does that mean we do not have the desire to sin? No. Does it mean that we will never have a wrong thought again? No. What it means is that we should have a stronger desire to live for God than living for ourselves.

Putting on Our New Nature in Christ

Anyone who thinks that they are better than anyone else is determining this based on their own deeds. Sure, when you compare yourself to everyone else in this world, based on our works we are all still sinners, but when our life is compared to those who do not have a relationship with God, it makes all the difference in our lives from being directed by the Holy Spirit or being lead astray by the things of this world.

For those who hear the Holy Spirit in their life, the change happens. But why? Because our idea of pleasing ourselves first is replaced by putting God first and ourselves second. We put away our selfish desires and put on the new life that comes through Jesus Christ.

The Proof of Christ in Our Actions.

What about our lives? Do we consider our lives in second place when it comes to God?

> James 1:22-24 "But prove yourselves doers of the word, and not merely hearers who delude themselves. 23 For if anyone is a hearer of the word and not a doer, he is like a man who looks at his natural face in a mirror; 24 for once he has looked at himself and gone away, he has immediately forgotten what kind of person he was."

The word "prove" in the original Greek is poiataste, (POI A TASTE), one who is a doer, a maker, a producer, author. How do you prove something? Do you remember as kids we would say that we could do something, like jumping a ramp on a bicycle, climbing a tall tree, or doing an unusual stunt like jumping out of a barn or jumping off a cliff? When we said we could do it, what did the other kids say to us? Prove it! If you were going to do something, you would have to back it up by doing whatever you said you could do.

What about your Christian life? Do your actions back up what you say? How much of your life is backed up by what you say? How much of our life is showing ourselves believers in Jesus Christ? It is one thing to call yourself a Christian, but where is the fruit?

> John 15:16-17 "You did not choose Me but I chose you and appointed you that you would go and bear fruit, and that your fruit would remain, so that whatever you ask of the Father in My name He may give to you. 17 This I command you, that you love one another."

Jesus tells us to carry out His Word in our life with the same word given in James 1 meaning to prove that we have a changed life. The idea to prove his love is to demonstrate the very love of God in the things we do and say as we model the life of Jesus Christ. As William Shakespeare most eloquently phrased in the play Hamlet, "To be or not to be that is the question".

For us, as believers, there is no question about our life. If you are a Christian, then people should be able to look for and find the fruit in your life.

PUTTING ON THE NEWNESS OF LIFE IN CHRIST

We all understand the need for the daily changing of the clothes we wear. Why? Because they are dirty, stinky, soiled, and grungy. How can you tell if a person has not showered or changed their clothes in several days? They stink, they smell, and there are stains all over their clothing. How can a person tell of a new life in Christ?

2 Corinthians 5:17 says, "Therefore if anyone is in Christ, he is a new creature; the old things passed away; behold, new things have come."

What is the evidence of Jesus working and living in our lives? A disciple of Jesus Christ will produce spiritual fruit. John 15:8 Jesus said, "My Father is glorified by this, that you bear much fruit, and so prove to be my disciples." Jesus also said in Matthew 7:20, "So then, you will know them by their fruits.

Our life is more than just talking the talk, it is also walking the walk. This is something to live for. Think of our life in this way, what if our life was shown the same way in which we wear a t-shirt? What if our life was said exactly the way we were and thought inside? What would your t-shirt say?

WHILE I WAIT

There was a time in my life that I had just left a ministry and I was seeking God's direction for the next church that he was calling me to. While waiting, I found a job working at Chick fil a. I was thirty-six years old supporting my family by working at Chick fil a. At this point in my life, I told God, (yeah, I know, *I told God*). I said, "God you have made a mistake, this is not where I am supposed to be". I guess you could say, I was upset and puzzled why God had put me there. In my mind I was saying, this wasn't the place I expected to be at, and this is not what I was supposed to be doing. I thought this is not where I could be the most effective for God. Do you see the selfishness I had before God? Have you ever said and acted this way before God? It wasn't until one day when one of the staff asked me a question, "Do you believe demons are real?" From that question on, God had allowed me to share the truth about who he was and what he had done through Christ. Time after time they would ask questions about God and the world around us.

It was a couple of months later after answering all their questions and sharing God's word that the person gave their life to Jesus. Not only that, but someone else had seen the change in the person's life who I had been witnessing too and within a couple of weeks, the other person gave their heart to Jesus. The reason this happened was that they saw something different in that person who came to know Jesus as their Savior. God had not only allowed me to be a testimony for him but also allowed me to see several people come to know the Lord as their personal savior. Why? Because God showed through my life. What about your life? Can others see Jesus in you?

GOD WORKS WHERE WE ARE

God does not just work in a church, he does not just work at an outreach event, he works in us and through us exactly where we are. God works in us where He plants us. Did you miss that? Because I sure did. Who are you being a witness to at work? Who are you being a witness to in your neighborhood? Who are you being a witness to in your grocery store? Are you sharing Jesus through your actions and words? James 1:22 does not say, prove yourselves doers of the word, at church, it says prove yourself at all times.

> 2 Timothy 4:2 "preach the word; be ready in season and out of season; reprove, rebuke, exhort, with great patience and instruction."

What happens with our life when we are merely hearers of God's Word and do not carry out the message through our life?

> James 1:23-25 "For if anyone is a hearer of the word and not a doer, he is like a man who looks at his natural face in a mirror; 24 for once he has looked at himself and gone away, he has immediately forgotten what kind of person he was. 25 But one who looks intently at the perfect law, the law of liberty, and abides by it, not having become a forgetful hearer but an effectual doer, this man will be blessed in what he does."

Have you ever looked at your reflection in a metal spoon? In the reflection of the metal spoon, the image is strange, warped, and imperfect.

Mirrors in Paul's time were made of metal and you could not see a very accurate reflection of yourself, it might have been the same as looking into a metal spoon. Today we have mirrors that can display exactly what we look like. Scary sometimes I know.

Some mirrors are even magnified to show the finer details of your face.

In the mirror, you can see yourself, your image, and what you look like. The same can be said of our Christian life and God's Word. As we are called to live the Christian life, we need to look into the mirror of God's Word, the true mirror, and see who we are and how we are compared to the image of Christ. We need to examine ourselves and ask the question: Am I being all that God has called me to be? Am I allowing the Lord to mold me? Am I doing my best and am I giving my best?

God's Word is an intimately detailed look at who we are, why we exist, and how we are called to live. When we look into God's mirror we may find; feelings, thoughts, problems, and attitudes that we have not allowed God to transform in us. We need to allow God to impact the way we walk, the way we talk, the way we think, and the way we act. Christianity is the newness of life we have in Jesus Christ, not the works of our old self. It is not a matter of being a better you, but Christ living through you.

> James 1:26-27 "If anyone thinks himself to be religious, and yet does not bridle his tongue but deceives his own heart, this man's religion is worthless. 27 Pure and undefiled religion in the sight of our God and Father is this: to visit orphans and widows in their distress, and to keep oneself unstained by the world."

SHINE FOR GOD

Growing up in the city, I never really got to see the stars at night. I knew they were there, but because of the light pollution of the city, I could never really see them. But no matter how much light there was in the city, I could always see the moon. I cannot tell you how many times I go out and look up at the moon. Especially when the moon was full and it pierced through the cold, dark night.

Think about this, the only reason we can see the moon is that it reflects the light from the sun. Imagine that, we would never have the ability to see the beautiful moon at night if it did not reflect the light of the sun. The same can be said for us as Christians. God calls for us to be so much more than a mere sign on the road of life, he calls for us to be the very model of himself to this world. Jesus said, Matthew 5:16 "Let your light shine before others". No one lights a lamp just to hide it under a basket. A lamp is meant to be placed on a stand to give light to everything around it. Whether you're timid or outgoing, you are called to be a light to the people around you. For us, the glory is always pointing back to the light source.

When Jesus said, "Let your light shine before others," that wasn't the whole sentence. He went on to give the reason why it's important to shine: "so that they may see your good works and give glory to your Father who is in heaven" (Matthew 5:16b). Our goal should never be to bring recognition to ourselves but to bring glory to God. It's a matter of the heart.

If you have ever seen the "Passion of the Christ" Jim Caviezel was the actor who played Jesus Christ. He said that when they were on the set, he did not want people to see him as the actor, but that he wanted people to see Jesus. The whole time he played the role, he said he did not feel like he was worthy to play the part of Jesus. Jim said, "I kept reflecting on all my sins."

How do you see your life in Jesus Christ? Is He just part of your life or is he all of your life? Who are you in Christ? Take a moment and examine your heart before the Lord and see if you match up to who God's Word said we are to be.

5

Examine your Heart

Have you ever put a jigsaw puzzle together and when you are almost done, you come down to the last piece of the puzzle and find that it is missing? A jigsaw puzzle is a set of interlocking pieces that when assembled produce a complete picture, often of nature, landscapes, or a work of art. Each piece is unique. When each piece is fit together it contributes to the entire puzzle. But what happens when the last piece is missing? You cannot complete the picture. Are we missing that piece of the puzzle that allows us to be complete in Christ?

Life is like a puzzle with a variety of pieces interlocking to create a masterpiece. It is interesting that as we study the Bible, each verse we study seems to bring us full circle to display a more complete image of God.

Throughout the previous chapters, we have learned how to become the picture of Christ in our lives, how to overcome temptations and trials with joy, how to trust in God for everything and rely on him alone, deal with our hearts, our desires, and our temptations, and using the mirror of scripture to see who we are portraying and making changes where they are needed. All of these are steps to becoming more like Christ.

God looks at the condition of our hearts. Just like the puzzle we often have missing pieces in our life that leave us incomplete. God in his perfect process of bringing us into the image of the stature of his Son, is looking to fill those areas in our lives that fall short.

When was the last time you pointed out the flaws in others' lives before you saw the ones in your own life? You may have heard the saying, "Those who live in glass houses should not throw stones". What a practical saying, but not very realistic. Why are we so quick to judge people?

We judge the way a person looks, speaks, their attitude, and the way they dress. Do you remember how we used to do this as kids? If the one kid dressed funny or had different clothes, kids would tend to stay away from them. If they were different the other kids would tend to pick them last for games. Children often judged the person by how they did things. The sad thing is that some people have never gotten over this stage in their life where they judge people. Have you heard people say phrases like; "They don't know what they're doing", "They have no clue" "If they only would do_____, (fill in the blank), their life would be better".

If a person who was homeless or someone who dressed differently walked into our church what would your reaction be? Most people would probably avoid them because they are dressed differently. The strange thing is that you could take the same person and put on different clothes and then people would welcome them and accept them.

LOVE PROMOTES GOD

I think we get lost in this idea that I feel loved when you do something for me. Or I will love you only when you do it first. This is the opposite of what God calls us to do as Christians. The world says "Me first" where Jesus' love says, "Others first".

We live in a society that says, "love me first and I'll love you if I feel like it". I get so frustrated at the legalism of certain churches that says, "You must wear this to come to our church", "You must act like this to come to our church", "You must be this denomination to attend here". When did Jesus ever kick someone away for not being worthy of being in His presence? When did Jesus ever reject someone for the clothes that they wore?

What is God most concerned with? Our heart! Even in the book of 1 Samuel 16. Samuel is commanded by God to go to the home of Jesse to anoint one of his sons as king of Israel. Samuel goes in and sees Eliab, the oldest son, and is convinced that this will be the next king of Israel because of his appearance. He was tall and had fair features and Samuel thought Eliab had the same qualities as Saul who was tall and handsome. Samuel thought this was God's man because of how he looked. But then God showed Samuel the qualities he was looking for.

> 1 Samuel 16:7 "But the LORD said to Samuel, "Do not look at his appearance or at the height of his stature, because I have rejected him; **for God sees not as man sees, for man looks at the outward appearance, but the LORD looks at the heart."**

LOVE DOES NOT JUDGE

> 1 Corinthians 13:4-8 "Love is patient, love is kind and is not jealous; love does not brag and is not arrogant, 5 does not act unbecomingly; it does not seek its own, is not provoked, does not take into account a wrong suffered, 6 does not rejoice in unrighteousness, but rejoices with the truth; 7 bears all things, believes all things, hopes all things, endures all things. 8 Love never fails;"

Often people like to point out our failures before they begin the love process. We all make mistakes, but why is it that we jump to a process of anger rather than forgiveness? Why do we pick up stones to throw rather than open our arms of love?

> Matthew 7:1-5 "Do not judge so that you will not be judged. 2"For in the way you judge, you will be judged; and by your standard of measure, it will be measured to you. 3"Why do you look at the speck that is in your brother's eye, but do not notice the log that is in your own eye? 4"Or how can you say to your brother, 'Let me take the speck out of your eye,' and behold, the log is in your own eye? 5"You hypocrite, first take the log out of your own eye, and then you will see clearly to take the speck out of your brother's eye."

At what point do we look at our own lives and see all the faults that we have, all the sins that we face, and all the reasons why Jesus had to die for us? It's so easy to point fingers at others, yet how are we at showing the love of God? When we acknowledge our own need for grace, compassion, and mercy, this motivates us to show these same virtues to others; to love them as God loves us. The command for believers is to glorify God with our life.

> 1 Corinthians 10:31-33 "Whether, then, you eat or drink or whatever you do, do all to the glory of God. 32Give no offense either to Jews or to Greeks or to the church of God; 33just as I also please all men in all things, not seeking my own profit but the profit of the many, so that they may be saved."

OUR ACTIONS REFLECT GOD'S LOVE

God often speaks to our love versus our prejudice.

> John 13:34-35 "I am giving you a new commandment, that you love one another; just as I have loved you, that you also love one another. 35 By this all people will know that you are My disciples: if you have love for one another."

The definition of prejudice is a preconceived opinion that is not based on reason or experience. Prejudice is preferential bias, and it can be either favorable or unfavorable. But the term prejudice most often refers to a negative opinion, not based on fact or experience, formed without just grounds or sufficient knowledge. People have a natural tendency to show prejudice toward anyone different. But what has God commanded us in scripture?

In Matthew, when Jesus was asked what is the greatest commandment, he stated first the love for God and then loving others.

> Matthew 22:36-40 "Teacher, which is the great commandment in the Law?" 37 And He said to him, "'You shall love the Lord your God with all your heart, and with all your soul, and with all your mind.' 38 This is the great and foremost commandment. 39 The second is like it, 'You shall love your neighbor as yourself.'"

God never said, love others if they are like you, or act like you. He never said only love others if they agree with your opinions, the verse clearly states, you love.

We often have our own agenda in life. How I plan to live, how I think, and the way I feel. The problem with this way of thinking is that at what point did you consider what would honor God and give him the glory? Now the question should be asked, "Is my life-giving God the glory or myself?" I mean really take a look at your life. What is your life really about? Our preconceived opinion that is not based on reason, or experience, is usually based on how I feel.

When we think of prejudice, we often see the images that are so common on TV today; riots, protests, outspoken politicians, and civil leaders claiming some type of wrongdoing while promoting discord and rhetoric.

We need to look at prejudice, not from the lens of a TV camera or the pages of a newspaper, but instead, we need to look at the prejudice within ourselves. How do our perceptions line up with how we are called to live according to the scripture? How do we decide if we are going to love or if we are going to hate?

COMPARING OUR LIFE TO SCRIPTURE

When we are sick there is technology in the medical field that has done a marvelous job of looking at the inside of our bodies. When you break your leg, an x-ray machine can see the fracture. When something is wrong with our organs, a magnetic resonance imaging machine, also called an MRI, uses large magnets and radio waves to generate images of the organs in the body. The MRI scan can diagnose a variety of conditions, from torn ligaments to tumors. A computerized axial tomography, known as a CAT scan, detects diseases and conditions, and the positron emission tomography (PET) scan is an imaging test that helps reveal how your tissues and organs are functioning.

We have all these different types of equipment to see the inside workings of our body, but how does one look at the heart and the will of a person? There is only one who can do that, God. David has repeatedly said through the book of Psalms that God knows our hearts.

> Psalm 139:23-24 "Search me, O God, and know
> my heart; Try me and know my anxious thoughts;
> 24 And see if there be any hurtful way in me, And
> lead me in the everlasting way."

> Psalm 26:2 "Examine me, O LORD, and try me;
> Test my mind and my heart."

> Psalm 44:21 "Would God not find this out? For
> He knows the secrets of the heart."

Over and over again David asks God to search his heart and to show him anything that is not what God desires of him. Why do we not pray the same thing that David prayed? Because we have those hidden agendas, pride, despair, and loneliness, and that constant sin that plagues us that we want to hang onto.

Examining our life is essential to our growth as a believer. Seeing our sins and failings will make it possible for us to confess, repent, find forgiveness, and grow in grace. It is by these steps that we move forward in the Christian life. If we can't see our failings, we can't make progress.

> James 1:10-11 "For whoever keeps the whole law
> and yet stumbles in one point, he has become
> guilty of all. 11 For He who said, "Do not commit
> adultery," also said, "Do not commit murder."
> Now if you do not commit adultery, but do
> commit murder, you have become a transgressor
> of the law.

No matter how good you are, no matter how well you are dressed, God is looking for the heart that says, "God, I want you to change my heart".

How do I compare to the image of Jesus? Why are we so good at carrying the gavel and playing judge and yet we forget to look into the mirror? For some of us, maybe we don't want to see what is in the mirror. How can you show the love of God when partiality is part of your thinking, how you act, and what you do? To break God's law is sin and to break even one part of the law is to break the whole law. Since God's law will be the standard by which everyone will be judged, shouldn't we live in light of that coming judgment?

We tend to pat ourselves on the back at what a great job we are doing as Christians, "but if you show partiality, you are committing sin and are convicted by the law as transgressors." We have the gavel in our hand waiting to pronounce judgment on people, but it is God and God alone who is our judge.

> James 4:12 says, "There is only one Lawgiver and
> Judge, the One who is able to save and to destroy;
> but who are you who judge your neighbor?"

If a man is guilty of murder and he goes before the court of law to be judged, it does not matter if he has been a faithful husband and father if he has never had a traffic ticket, has never robbed a bank or has never beaten up his neighbor. All that matters is, did he commit murder? If so, he is guilty of breaking the law, he is guilty of murder.

Jesus said John 5:24 "Truly, truly, I say to you, he who hears My word and believes Him who sent Me, has eternal life, and does not come into judgment, but has passed out of death into life."

LIVING A LIFE WORTHY OF THE NAME OF JESUS

The apostle Paul states clearly in Romans. 8:1"Therefore there is now no condemnation to those who are in Christ Jesus." Scripture clearly shows that Christ bore the punishment that we deserve for our sins. If we have trusted in Him, we will not face God's eternal wrath at the final judgment (the "great white throne" judgment, Rev. 20:11-15). Because of Jesus Christ, we are declared not guilty before God.

Even though we do not need to fear that awful judgment for our sins, if we are in Christ, we will appear before God to give account for our deeds.

> 2 Cor. 5:10 "For we must all appear before the judgment seat of Christ, so that each one may be recompensed for his deeds in the body, according to what he has done, whether good or bad."

Through Jesus Christ, our sins have been judged and removed from us. But our lives as believers will undergo the Lord's heart-level evaluation. Those things that were done out of love for Christ and his glory will be rewarded. Those things that were done out of selfish motives are worthless in God's sight and will be burned as wood, hay, and stubble (1 Cor. 3:11-15).

GLORIFYING JESUS IN OUR LIFE

What needs to happen is that we need to think more about who we are in Christ, how our life matches up to the standard of Jesus Christ, and being the love of Christ more than being the judge of other people and their lives. We need to be supporting, helping, encouraging, and declaring the love of Jesus rather than the ones casting the first stones. Our lives need to be about living and showing the love of Jesus.

When people see you, who do they see? When people meet you, will they see Jesus first in your life?

6

A Faith that Works

At a high ropes course near me, there is an obstacle called the "leap of faith". Let me see if I can explain the obstacle. In the middle between two trees is a telephone pole that stands by itself, jetting up thirty feet into the air. At the top of the pole, there is a trapeze bar that is three feet away from the top of the pole. To complete this obstacle, you must climb a thirty-foot telephone pole, stand on the top of the pole, which has no handhold, and jump off the pole to reach the trapeze bar.

You have to take a leap of faith.

For many, they look at the pole and say, "no way". Just reading this may have you scared at the thought. Just the thought of climbing the pole is terrifying enough, but then to reach the top of the pole and stand on top of it while looking out over the horizon. Another breaking point. To think that now there is a small bar that you need to jump off of the pole to reach a bar three feet away, not happening. Even though all of this sounds terrifying, remember that you have a harness and a guide rope strapped around you to keep you from falling, why would you lack faith? Many may be asking, "why would you do this"?

What is Faith? Faith is the result of what we believe God's Word said is true. Hebrews 11:1 tells us that faith is "being sure of what we hope for and certain of what we do not see."

Perhaps no other component of the Christian life is more important than faith. Think about it, we cannot purchase it, sell it, or give it to our friends. You cannot just say, "Here is my faith, go and be happy".

What is faith and what role does faith play in the Christian life?

The definition of faith is "a belief in, devotion to, or trust in somebody or something, especially without logical proof." It also defines faith as "belief in and devotion to God."

> James 2:14-17 "What use is it, my brethren, if someone says he has faith but he has no works? Can that faith save him? 15 If a brother or sister is without clothing and in need of daily food, 16 and one of you says to them, "Go in peace, be warmed and be filled," and yet you do not give them what is necessary for their body, what use is that? 17 Even so faith, if it has no works, is dead, being by itself."

Faith is not just the substance of things hoped for or the evidence of things unseen or how believers can obtain a good report. Faith is much more than that, faith is the basis and the foundation of our Christianity. The Bible says, "Without faith, we cannot please God." Without our faith, we cannot totally surrender to God.

TAKING THE LEAP

I love to take adventures. Most of the time it is doing something I have never done before. Rock climbing, rappelling, and zip-lining are some just to name a few. Each one is an exciting experience that requires me to put my faith in a rope that is attached to me to keep me from falling. Defying your brain's normalized laws of gravity, rappelling successfully and with much control can involve putting your body at a 90-degree angle and walking down a massive steep rock backward. What is the scariest part of rappelling? It is the first step over the edge, why you may ask because it is at that point you put all of your faith into a rope that is supporting you. It is that first step into the unknown where you cannot depend upon yourself to keep yourself from falling. It is putting your complete trust in the rope that is holding you.

The same faith that it takes to put trust in the rope is also the same faith we put in God when it comes to our life by trusting him completely. Faith is the action done in response to God's work. Faith isn't a feeling, and it's not a supernatural force to get God to give us what we desire.

God makes it extremely clear that faith is a gift from God, not because we deserve it, not because we have earned it, or are worthy to have it.

> Ephesians 2:8 "For by grace you have been saved
> through faith; and that not of yourselves, it is the
> gift of God"

It is not from ourselves; it is from God. So many people get it wrong when they believe that it can be obtained by our power or our free will. Faith is simply given to us by God, along with His grace and mercy, according to His holy plan and purpose, and because of that, he gets all the glory, not us.

OUR DEMONSTRATION OF FAITH

We believe in God's existence by faith. Faith is only as strong as the thing to which it is anchored. What faith does is demolish, destroy, dismantle, and bring down all the barriers to our works that are the obstacles to living a life destined and ordained by God.

Did you know that the African impala can jump to a height of over ten feet and cover a distance of greater than thirty feet? In our area, we have white-tailed deer which can jump up to eight feet. Yet, the interesting fact about the impala is that it can be kept in an enclosure in any zoo with a three-foot wall. Wonder why? The African impala will not jump over something if they cannot see where their feet will fall. Faith is the ability to trust what we cannot see.

When I was a youth leader, we used to take a group of youth white water rafting. These were not the small lazy rivers you float down; they were the class three and four size hydraulics and rapids that would most likely throw you out of the boat and into the raging waters. If you had never been rafting before it was quite an experience. Along the journey, we were guaranteed to hit large size boulders protruding from the water and at some point, in the journey, we found ourselves outside of the boat and racing down the river without the raft.

Sometimes, in the process of our life, we get thrown into raging rapids. At that point what are we going to cling onto when we are in the waters of life, the hydraulics that wants to take us down, as the waves which keep crashing over our heads? This is where faith comes into our life.

Faith is a verb, it requires action. What do you cling to when you are in the storms of life? What do you do when you are hanging by a rope? Faith requires dependence on God, who when the troubles of life come, and they will come, will help you through them.

Has our faith become just a ritual? A response that has no results? Faith gives us the courage to perceive and do the right thing, to live a life pleasing to God. Sometimes we come against things that violate our core principles and we may not be able to speak up or stand up for what we know we should, but with the conviction and power of faith, we can stand up for our beliefs and consequently do the right thing.

HOPE IN HOPELESSNESS

How can we have hope when everything looks hopeless?

> Romans 5:3-5 "And not only this, but we also celebrate in our tribulations, knowing that tribulation brings about perseverance; 4 and perseverance, proven character; and proven character, hope; 5 and hope does not disappoint, because the love of God has been poured out within our hearts through the Holy Spirit who was given to us."

How easy is it for us to put hope in God when things are going well? How about when we come against something in our life that is out of our control? At what point do we allow our hope, to be put into effect, that strengthens our faith?

In Luke 8:43-44 we find a woman who had to take her faith and put it into action.

> Luke 8:43-44 "And a woman who had suffered a chronic flow of blood for twelve years, and could not be healed by anyone, 44 came up behind Him and touched the fringe of His cloak, and immediately her bleeding stopped."

Here comes a woman whose only hope is Jesus. This woman, who we see in this interaction with Jesus, has had a bleeding disease for twelve years.

> Mark 5:25-27 "A woman who had had a hemorrhage for twelve years, 26 and had endured much at the hands of many physicians, and had spent all that she had and was not helped at all, but instead had become worse 27 after hearing about Jesus, she came up in the crowd behind Him and touched His cloak."

Mark gives us a little more insight into this woman's life. The disease had taken all her strength away and all the money she had paid doctors to heal her problem. She had tried everything anyone had told her and nothing helped. All she wanted to do is reach Jesus, her last hope. Her last hope would require her to have faith. As she tries to reach Jesus, she knows she does not have to be first in line, but only to touch the hem of Jesus' garment. This woman believed that if she could just touch Jesus' cloak that she will have gotten close enough to him to be healed. In her mind, all that is necessary is to touch His robe. She doesn't have to touch His hand, just His garment.

How many people still think like this today? How many of us believe in the extended power of Jesus' reach? This was an example of faith in action.

An old Scotsman operated a little rowboat for transporting passengers. One day a passenger noticed that the good old man had carved on one oar, the word "Faith," and on the other oar the word "Works." Curiosity led him to ask the meaning of this. The old man, being a well-balanced Christian and glad of the opportunity for testimony, said, "I will show you. "So, he dropped the oar called Faith and held the other oar (Works), up in the boat and they just went around in circles. Then he dropped the "Works" oar and began to ply the oar called Faith, and the little boat just went around in circles again— this time the other way around, but still in a circle. After this demonstration the old man picked up Faith and Works and using both oars together, sped swiftly over the water, explaining to his inquiring passenger, "You see, that is the way it is in the Christian life. Dead works without faith are useless, and "faith without works is dead" also, getting you nowhere. But faith and works pulling together make for safety, progress, and blessing." (Paul Lee Tan, Encyclopedia of 7700 Illustrations: A Treasury of Illustrations, Anecdotes, Facts and Quotations for Pastors, Teachers and Christian Workers (Garland TX: Bible Communications, 1996, c1979).

Can God still do miracles today? Absolutely! But where is our faith? Is it in our works or is it in the power of the almighty God?

The problem I think we deal with is that our faith and trust in God falls flat. Why? Because God cannot do it? Because the problems in our lives are too big for God? If you believe he can do it, where is your faith?

There is an old saying, "If you're praying for rain, bring the umbrella." The problem is not whether can God do it, the problem is that we need to stop working by our efforts and start trusting God more.

When you pray are you expecting to see results or do, you just offer it to God and hope he answers it? Maybe our prayer needs to become, "God let my faith be made sight." We believe God can, but in our minds, we question the work of God. How will God work? We don't know. In what way will he work? We don't know. The one thing I know is that, for believers, God hears us and wants to work on our behalf.

> John 14:12-14 "Truly, truly I say to you, the one who believes in Me, the works that I do, he will do also; and greater works than these he will do; because I am going to the Father. 13And whatever you ask in My name, this I will do, so that the Father may be glorified in the Son. 14If you ask Me anything in My name, I will do it."

GOD'S WILL

There are two parts of the will of God. First, there is the unconditional sovereign will of God when God has determined that something will happen according to His perfect and sovereign will. The second is his conditional will, which he will change, but we need to ask.

> Philippians 4: 4-6 "Rejoice in the Lord always; again I will say, rejoice! 5 Let your gentle spirit be known to all people. The Lord is near. 6 Do not be anxious about anything, but in everything by prayer and pleading with thanksgiving let your requests be made known to God."

There are some times when God may say "no" because we ask with the wrong motives, and there are also times he says "yes" because he wants us to have what we ask for. But understanding, how he answers our prayers is still up to him. He loves us. He wants to work in our lives if we will just let him.

I guess a big question for each of us is how do we incorporate our faith, that which we know to be true about God, and apply it to our lives? Knowing what faith is, is one thing. Having faith and putting your faith to work is another.

Think about it like this, if a man or woman possessing the qualifications and licensures to practice medicine went around calling themselves a doctor, but never treated anyone and even refused to help someone in need of emergency care, is that person a doctor? Maybe on paper, but not in life. He or she is nothing more than someone with knowledge and potential or rather, wasted knowledge and potential.

YOUR LAST RESORT

You may be on the very precipice of life, right at the very edge of things, or you may feel you are buried in a deep dark unreachable place. You may even think of Jesus as a kind of last resort and many people approach faith in this way. No matter what is going on around you, don't trust in your way, we need to trust in Yahweh. God is a God of Hope. Know this, there is power in the name of Jesus.

> Ephesians 3:16-21 "that He would grant you, according to the riches of His glory, to be strengthened with power through His Spirit in the inner self, 17 so that Christ may dwell in your hearts through faith; and that you, being rooted and grounded in love, 18 may be able to comprehend with all the saints what is the width and length and height and depth, 19 and to know the love of Christ which surpasses knowledge, that you may be filled to all the fullness of God. 20 Now to Him who is able to do far more abundantly beyond all that we ask or think, according to the power that works within us, 21 to Him be the glory in the church and in Christ Jesus to all generations forever and ever. Amen."

I understand that sometimes our circumstances can be a crushing blow to our faith. The pain can be so great that it's hard to keep hoping and believing. We just want to run away from whatever the circumstances are because we're afraid we will be crushed. However, Paul reminds us that as Christians, we are to keep hoping in Jesus. He is writing your story and it is a story of hope. Hebrews 12:2 says, "looking only at Jesus, the originator and perfecter of the faith, who for the joy set before Him endured the cross, despising the shame, and has sat down at the right hand of the throne of God."

You are part of HIS-STORY! Even in the good and bad that we face in life.

PUTTING FAITH INTO PRACTICE

How do I take what I know to be true about God and his words and his promises and let them be effective in my situation? Keep praying and asking God, according to his Word, to work in your situation. Do we believe that he is going to work? Yes. But the work may be in our situation or the work may be in us as we accept our situation.

> Mark 11: 22-23 "22 And Jesus answered and *said to them, "Have faith in God. 23 Truly I say to you, whoever says to this mountain, 'Be taken up and thrown into the sea,' and does not doubt in his heart, but believes that what he says is going to happen, it will be granted to him.""

One of the most important questions we can ask is; where is the bedrock foundation of our faith? It is our faith in God and his ability to work. We tend to focus on the size of the mountain that is in front of us, instead of the power that God gives through his Holy Spirit to overcome those mountains. Think about Jesus' disciples. After Jesus had died, rose again, and went back into heaven, how were the disciple able to continue to do miracles? By their power? No, it was by God's power, the Holy Spirit, working through them.

> Acts 3:6-8 "But Peter said, "I do not have silver and gold, but what I do have I give to you: In the name of Jesus Christ the Nazarene, walk!" 7And grasping him by the right hand, he raised him up; and immediately his feet and his ankles were strengthened. 8And leaping up, he stood and began to walk; and he entered the temple with them, walking and leaping and praising God."

To put faith in God means you must put faith in God's Word, God's will, and in God's character. When David met Goliath on the battlefield, what allowed David to be victorious? His skill with a sling, his strength, his battle strategy? No, it was the power of God. David wasn't focusing on the size of the mountain; he was focusing on the power of his God. For believers, what is faith? It is to believe in the power of God and take action on the unseen. It is not about religion; it is about your relationship with the source of all power.

Understand that faith without action is ineffective. Our faith must be based on hearing and believing what God has said in His Word. Faith is a matter of us hearing his word, believing in it, and then acting upon it. Faith is not passive; it requires us to take some kind of action. Moving mountains is not accomplished by mustering up enough faith. It is done by trusting God to move the mountains by God's power.

You may be asking yourself, "How do I know if something I'm asking for is God's will?" The answer to the question is that we do not know. We do not know whether it's God's sovereign will or not, but he has given us the privilege to come to him asking in prayer for it to be done and if it is His will to move in your prayer, he will give you confidence, a sense of assurance or a sense of peace upon your request.

> 1 John 5:14-15 "This is the confidence which we have before Him, that, if we ask anything according to His will, He hears us. 15 And if we know that He hears us in whatever we ask, we know that we have the requests which we have asked from Him."

God Prepares Us

When God is doing something big in your life, he has to do two things at the same time: preparing the thing that he is going to do and preparing you for the thing that He is doing.

Let me tell you, God can speak healing to someone with a cold or stage five cancer. Luke 1:37 says, "For nothing will be impossible with God." Do you believe that? I mean do you really believe that? Can God do the impossible thing in your life? Doubt and belief cannot exist together. You will give priority to one or the other. Do you believe in God and the power of His Word? Do you believe God can move in any situation in your life? We have this available power from God in our lives and yet, we fail to use it because we are trying to do things by our power instead of His.

FAITH TO MOVE MOUNTAINS

> James 2:18 "But someone may well say, "You have faith and I have works; show me your faith without the works, and I will show you my faith by my works."

A small congregation in the foothills of the smoky mountains in Tennessee had built a new sanctuary on a piece of land willed to them by a church member. Ten days before the new church was to open, the local building inspector informed the pastor that the parking lot was inadequate for the size of the building. Until the church doubled the size of the parking lot, they would not be able to use the new sanctuary. Unfortunately, the church with its undersized lot had used every inch of their land except for the mountain against which it had been built. In order to build more parking spaces, they would have to move the mountain out of the back yard.

The pastor announced on Sunday morning that he would meet that evening with all members who had "mountain moving faith." They would hold a prayer session asking God to remove the mountain from the backyard and to somehow provide enough money to have it paved and painted before the scheduled opening dedication service the following week. At the appointed time, twenty-four of the congregation's three hundred church members assembled for prayer. They prayed for nearly three hours. At ten o'clock the pastor said the final "Amen". "We'll open next Sunday as scheduled," he assured everyone. "God has never let us down before, and I believe He will be faithful this time too."

The next morning, as he was working in his study there, came a loud knock at his door. When he called "come in", a rough-looking construction foreman appeared, removing his hard hat as he entered. "Excuse me, Reverend. I'm from a local Construction Company over in the next county. We're building a huge shopping mall. We need some fill dirt. Would you be willing to sell us a chunk of that mountain behind the church? We'll pay you for the dirt we remove and pave all the exposed area free of charge if we can have it right away. We can't do anything else until we get the dirt in and allow it to settle properly."

The little church was dedicated the next Sunday as originally planned and there were far more members with "mountain moving faith" on opening Sunday than there had been the previous week. (Unknown author)

Let me ask you, "Would you have shown up for that prayer meeting?" There is a big difference between someone who says they believe and someone who follows Jesus' commands. Jesus said in John 14:15 "If you love Me, you will obey my commands.". He also said in John 15:10 "If you keep My commands, you will abide in my love, just as I have kept My Father's commandments and abide in His love."

FAITH EXPECTS GOD TO WORK

There are two keywords we must grasp when we talk about faith, belief, and abide. The original Greek in the Bible for "believe" is, pisteuó (pist-yoo'-o). It means to have faith in; an expectation that God is able and will do as He says.

In today's society, the term faith comes to mean nothing more than believing what you want and living in the world, and being no different from everyone around you. Many people today use the words faith and belief interchangeably. But is there a difference between these words in the Bible?

As Christians, we must strive for living faith. Living faith is our belief in God demonstrated by good works according to His laws and commandments. If we believe that God exists, we're on the same level of belief as the demons. Our belief should inspire us to be obedient to God and change the way we live our life. When we truly have faith it is seen in our increase and growth in our relationship with God. If we believe in God yet do not live according to his word, that is not faith, it is religion.

Religion can lead us to the belief that our only duty as a Christian is to leave the world for an hour or so on a Sunday morning to go to church and then we can be assured that all our sins are forgiven. That I need no longer try to follow Christ, for cheap grace, has freed me from that."

> James 2:26 "For just as the body without the spirit
> is dead, so also faith without works is dead."

Faith and works go hand in hand. An empty faith equals a non-action-filled faith, which is not true faith, it is not saving faith, and it is nothing more than saying the words. Our faith in God and trust in Jesus must work in tandem with our actions.

Have you ever heard of the great tightrope walker, Charles Blondin? He was also known as the Great Blondin or "King of the High Wire". He was one of the greatest tightrope walkers of all time, and there are many legends told of feats he performed.

One of the most often shared stories was when Blondin crossed over Niagara Falls on a tightrope. Sometimes he was blindfolded, other times he would hang from the wire with only his legs. He crossed at night, he crossed with his body in shackles and he crossed carrying a table and chair, stopping in the middle to try to sit down and prop up his legs.

During one of his performances, he turned to his large audience, which included numerous reporters from various newspapers, and he asked them, "How many believe I can walk across this tightrope, over Niagara Falls, pushing a wheelbarrow?" People cheered loudly. They were sure the great Blondin could do it.

Then he asked, "How many believe I can push a wheelbarrow across the tightrope with a man sitting in it?" Again, there was a great response. Blondin then proceeded to point to a man in the audience who had been cheering in the audience, and said, "Okay, you get into the wheelbarrow." Needless to say, the man made a quick exit.

Blondin demonstrated that there is often a great difference between belief, the faith we say we have, and the action faith we have. People may say that they have faith, but there was no action behind what they said. Without the Spirit of God, we will always remain barren of fruit.

THE MEASURE OF OUR FAITH IN OUR WALK

If I were to say to you "I'm a home builder" and you ask me if I have ever built a home? The answer would be "No". Then what I say about being a home builder doesn't add up. If I were to say I was a mechanic, and you ask, "Have you ever worked on a car"? and I say, "No" then am I really a mechanic? My words have to line up with my actions.

The same can be said for our life as Christians. Our faith is in Jesus' accomplished work that makes the difference between a believer and the unsaved man or woman. The question we need to ask ourselves is, does our faith line up with what we say?

The measure of our faith is not in what we say, it is what we are willing to do with what we say. The cure for the lack of faith in a lukewarm Christian is to get busy and put our faith into action. If we were to put actions behind our words, then the world would have fewer reasons to call Christians hypocrites, but instead would be constantly talking about the miracles God has performed in and through us.

In 1893, engineer George Ferris built a machine that bears his name-the Ferris wheel. When it was finished, he invited a newspaper reporter to accompany him and his wife for the inaugural ride. It was a windy July day, so a stiff breeze struck the wheel with great force as it slowly began its rotation. Despite the wind, the wheel turned flawlessly. After one revolution, Ferris called for the machine to be stopped so that he, his wife, and the reporter could step out. In braving that one revolution on the windblown Ferris wheel, each occupant demonstrated genuine faith. Mr. Ferris began with the scientific knowledge that the machine would work and that it would be safe. Mrs. Ferris and the reporter believed the machine would work based on what the inventor had said. But only after the ride could it be said of all three that they had personal, experiential faith.

In the Christian life, faith and works go together like inhaling and exhaling. What happens when you take a deep breath and hold it? See how long you can go without breathing?

Have you ever taken a CPR class? What are the ABCs of CPR? Airway, breathing, and circulation. If any of these is not present in a victim, then most likely the person is dead or on their way to death.

Billy Graham said, "Faith is taking the Gospel in and works are taking the Gospel out." We cannot possibly have faith worth anything if we don't put our beliefs in action. "So also faith by itself, if it does not have works, is dead." (James 2:17)

What does "living out your faith" look like? It means that your life gives God glory. It is not a simple expression you say when you are around other Christians. Living out our faith means that this is who we are, what we do and it is the very nature of who you are in Christ.

You can't say to someone I held my breath and I haven't breathed in days. Why? Because you would be dead. If you do not breathe you die. The same is said of our Christian life, if you don't act on your belief in Christ your faith is dead. Dead faith doesn't work. Dead faith doesn't save. Dead faith only makes a mockery of living faith by claiming to be valid. It is not simply the claim of faith that counts but the practice of our faith.

THE RESULTS OF FAITH

What is the result of Faith? Take for instance Peter in the Bible. He was a unique man. He was considered the boldest of all the disciples. Peter was the type of person who did things that other people didn't have the nerve to do. Do you remember when Peter walked on the water?

Matthew 14:28 Peter said to Him, "Lord, if it is You, command me to come to You on the water." 29 And He said, "Come!" And Peter got out of the boat, and walked on the water and came toward Jesus. 30 But seeing the wind, he became frightened, and beginning to sink, he cried out, "Lord, save me!" 31 Immediately Jesus stretched out His hand and took hold of him, and said to him, "You of little faith, why did you doubt?"

When did Peter's faith begin? When he saw Jesus or when he acted on that belief in Jesus? Do you see the faith and the trust that Peter had in Jesus? Peter had the faith that said, He believed who Jesus said He was and Peter believed Jesus when He said, "come". How could Peter walk on the water? Because of the power of trusting completely in Jesus.

The result of faith is that we become the living proof of a God who is at work. We are considered God's workmanship and because of that, there has to be evidence in our life. There has to be a change in us as a result of Jesus working. You can't say "Jesus came into my heart", and there is no difference. The result of Jesus coming into your life will be evidenced by your works, actions, and lifestyle.

> Ephesians 2:8-10 "For by grace you have been
> saved through faith; and that not of yourselves,
> it is the gift of God; 9not as a result of works,
> so that no one may boast. 10For we are His
> workmanship, created in Christ Jesus for good
> works, which God prepared beforehand so that
> we would walk in them."

How do you know someone is alive? They have a heartbeat, they have blood pressure, and they are breathing. How do you tell if a person has gone from death to life in Christ? You can tell it by heart, you can tell by the speech, you can tell by their actions. If a believer is truly alive, you will see the fruits.

What is the result of your faith? Is it that you just attend church regularly? Is it that you give a tithe to the Lord? Is it that you want to serve God with all your heart? Is it that you go out of your way to share Jesus with people? These are all things that should occur because of our faith, but they don't just end there. All of these should be a result of our faith in accordance with God's Word.

As God's workmanship, we were "created in Christ Jesus for good works, which God prepared beforehand so that we would walk in them." Remember faith requires action.

There was a group of skydivers who were getting together to jump out of the plane. A cameraman, who was a skydiver himself, was there to film this brilliant spectacle of the skydivers. The cameraman jumped first so that he could film each jumper as they began to jump out of the plane. One by one each fell from the plane and one by one each of the parachutes opened.

It was a beautiful shot for the camera guy. As the last skydiver opened his parachute the cameraman's camera went crazy. What had happened is that the cameraman was so preoccupied with the camera and the jump that he forgot to put on his parachute. He didn't even realize that when he jumped, he wasn't wearing a parachute. Because of this, the cameraman lost his life. No matter how much faith the cameraman had in his parachute, it did him no good if it wasn't attached to him.

7

The Power of the Word

ONCE UPON A TIME, A DONKEY FOUND A LION'S SKIN. HE TRIED IT on, strutted around, and frightened many animals. Soon a fox came along, and the donkey tried to scare him, too. But the fox, hearing the donkey's voice, said, "If you want to terrify me, you'll have to disguise your bray." Aesop's moral: Clothes may disguise a fool, but his words will give him away. (The Fables of Babrius, translated by Rev. John Davies, London 1860, P.178)

When we consider the words of Jesus in Matthew 12:34 we see why the tongue is given such extensive treatment. How we handle the tongue is a great indicator of our hearts before God.

> Matthew 12:35-37 "The good man brings out of his good treasure what is good; and the evil man brings out of his evil treasure what is evil. 36 "But I tell you that every careless word that people speak, they shall give an accounting for it in the day of judgment. 37 "For by your words you will be justified, and by your words, you will be condemned."

Our words give us away. It is amazing how our words show the very nature of our hearts. Proverbs 23:7 says, "For as a man thinks, so he is"

DEMONSTRATE YOUR LIFE WITH YOUR WORDS

Have you ever made yourself sick from constantly saying it to yourself? I don't feel good. Have you made yourself more fearful because you keep repeating to yourself that which made you afraid? Or lost courage because you kept saying to yourself you could not do something?

THERE IS POWER IN THE WORD OF GOD

How do we take the love of Christ to those outside of the walls of the church building, into the community, or into the world we live in? How do we communicate and show the lost world the love of Jesus Christ? By speaking in love.

How do we teach others the love of Jesus? Through our actions, through our love, and our words. Words are not simply sounds caused by air passing through our larynx, they are an expression of who we are.

Words are the most powerful force available to us. We can choose to use our word to help, to encourage, or to destroy those around us. Words have energy and power with the ability to help, to heal, to hinder, to hurt, to harm, to humiliate, and to humble. Words have real power; they do not only convey information. The power of our words can destroy one's spirit, even stir up hatred and violence. Words not only magnify wounds but inflict them directly. Of all the creatures on this planet, only man has the ability to communicate through the spoken word.

Did your mom ever say to you, "Sticks and stones will break my bones, but words will never hurt me" Of all the things my mom ever said to me, this is the one she got wrong. I still carry the wounds of hurtful words in my life. Proverb 18:21 tells us, "The tongue has the power of life and death."

In your own life, you need to ask yourself, "Am I using words to build up people or tear them down? Are they filled with hate or love, bitterness or blessing, complaining or compliments, lust or love, victory or defeat?

SPEAKING WITH THE POWER OF LOVE

When you look at your life, do others feel the power of Christs' love in your words? For believers it has to be more than mere words, it must be an expression of our faith and our belief in what God has commanded us to do.

> 1 John 3:18 "….let us not love with word or with tongue, but in deed and truth. 19We will know by this that we are of the truth, and will assure our heart before Him."

Is what we are saying influencing others for Christ? We are called to carry God's very word out to the world.

> Isaiah 55:11 "So will My word be which goes forth from My mouth; It will not return to Me empty, Without accomplishing what I desire, And without succeeding in the matter for which I sent it."

James 3:3-5 "Now if we put the bits into the horses' mouths so that they will obey us, we direct their entire body as well. 4 Look at the ships also, though they are so great and are driven by strong winds, are still directed by a very small rudder wherever the inclination of the pilot desires. 5 So also the tongue is a small part of the body, and yet it boasts of great things.

If we understand the importance of our words, how do we control what comes out of our mouths?

Most people understand a horse's bit and bridle. They are used to direct and control the horse's direction. We use the bridle to turn the horse's head the way we want to go. In the right hand, any of these bits can be a tool, but in the wrong hands, they can become a weapon as well causing damage instead of producing the desired outcome.

Also, when looking at the rudder on a ship. What does the rudder do? It turns the ship in the direction you want to go. Take for instance the largest cruise ship in the world. The largest Cruise ship in the world is One thousand, one hundred and eighty-eight feet long. To walk from the front of the ship to the back would take six minutes at a normal pace. It stands one hundred and eighteen feet taller than the Eiffel tower. To direct this beast of a ship it takes three sixty-foot rudder propellers. If you direct the rudders in the wrong direction, you can cause catastrophic disasters and death. So it is the same way with our tongue, small but powerful.

Our state requires months of training to drive a car, with

repeated practice and someone who rides along with you to ensure your safety. It is the same with the tongue. Children require training in the way they should go. Directing them how to speak. I find myself saying to my children all the time, "Say thank you", "Yes, mam", "no mam", "yes sir" and "no sir", "please and thank you". I take time to instruct them on how to be polite and respectful.

> James 3:6-8 "And the tongue is a fire, the very world of iniquity; the tongue is set among our members as that which defiles the entire body, and sets on fire the course of our life, and is set on fire by hell. 7 For every species of beasts and birds, of reptiles and creatures of the sea, is tamed and has been tamed by the human race. 8 But no one can tame the tongue; it is a restless evil and full of deadly poison."

This is so true. I have found that my words hurt. When I get into an argument, I choose to walk away and calm down, because I do not want my words to wound someone I love. My wife wants to make everything okay at that moment, but I can't because I want to calm down to make sure my words are used for uplifting and not tearing down.

James 1:19-20 says, "This you know, my beloved brethren. But everyone must be quick to hear, slow to speak and slow to anger; 20 for the anger of man does not achieve the righteousness of God."

See how this correlates with God's Word and being a witness for God? James 3:9-12, "With it, (speaking of the tongue) we bless our Lord and Father, and with it, we curse men, who have been made in the likeness of God; 10 from the same mouth come both blessing and cursing. My brethren, these things ought not to be this way. 11 Does a fountain send out from the same opening both fresh and bitter water? 12 Can a fig tree, my brethren, produce olives, or a vine produce figs? Nor can salt water produce fresh."

WHAT IS YOUR LIFE PRODUCING?

Jesus tells us that we are the light of the world. We reflect the love and goodness of our Savior in the way we live our lives. By our words and actions, we draw people to Christ and his precious gospel message. The Gospel message and our faith in Christ refers to dying to self and living for him, which is manifest in works of righteousness for the benefit of others and to the greater glory of God. It lets the beauty and love of Jesus be seen in us so that it flows out to others, in our actions and attitude.

> Luke 6:43-45 "For there is no good tree which produces bad fruit, nor, on the other hand, a bad tree which produces good fruit. 44"For each tree is known by its own fruit. For men do not gather figs from thorns, nor do they pick grapes from a briar bush. 45"The good man out of the good treasure of his heart brings forth what is good; and the evil man out of the evil treasure brings forth what is evil; for his mouth speaks from that which fills his heart."

What is your heart filled with today? To love in tongue only is contrasted with loving in spirit and in truth. The former is a dishonest and artificial love, while the other is a genuine godly love that is manifest in a life that cares for the concerns of others before one's own needs or wishes.

Does your life seek to bring praise to God or praise to man? If you are a believer and we know that God calls all who are saved by the blood of Christ to be His messengers, what message does your message bring? How do your words show love?

IMITATING GOD'S EXAMPLE

> Ephesians 5:1-4 "Therefore be imitators of God, as beloved children; 2and walk in love, just as Christ also loved you and gave Himself up for us, an offering and a sacrifice to God as a fragrant aroma. 3But immorality or any impurity or greed must not even be named among you, as is proper among saints; 4and there must be no filthiness and silly talk, or coarse jesting, which are not fitting, but rather giving of thanks."

Have you ever read "The Five Love Languages" by Gary Chapman? In his book, he lists the five different love languages that people have. One of those love languages is words of affirmation. One of the most important aspects of words of affirmation is being genuine with those words. People care most about the intentions and emotions behind those words, rather than the words themselves. I have come to realize that words of affirmation are not just the love language of some, but everyone.

In my past, I expressed my love for others via actions more than words. Words are easily given, but taking action to show your love for others requires a lot more time and effort. I realized that the words that I say make a difference to those around me. Do my actions and my words correspond to the love that God has given me and is it demonstrated through how I live my life?

Do your words fit with a life redeemed by Christ? As Believers, we ought to be growing more consistent in our speech. Redeemed speech and wisdom only come from the work of the Redeemer.

8

THE WISDOM OF LIVING
A GODLY LIFE

IN 2002 A DOCTOR WAS SUSPENDED FOR LEAVING A PATIENT ON the operating table midway through spinal surgery so he could deposit a check at his local bank. The state board of medicine said the doctor posed 'an immediate threat to the public health, safety, and welfare' after he left the patient with an open incision in his back. After his thirty-five-minute trip to the bank, the doctor returned to the operating room and finished the surgery. The doctor's excuse was that he had to get to the bank before it closed because he was in "a financial crisis," and had to pay overdue bills.

The doctor had plenty of knowledge and education, but it didn't necessarily bring along much wisdom.

LIVING IN THE WISDOM OF GOD

Being wise is not something you normally think about. For most of you, it comes naturally. How do we live in the wisdom of God's Word for a Godly life?

There are two kinds of wisdom in this world. There is heavenly wisdom and earthly wisdom. So how do we know the difference? How do we discern which is which? In a world where everyone has an opinion, everyone is ready to offer up advice, how do we know if what we are being told is wisdom from above, or wisdom from below?

WISDOM COMES FROM KNOWING THE TRUTH OF GOD

We know that knowledge is things that are learned and wisdom is that knowledge put into action. Knowledge is knowing the Word of God and wisdom is knowing how to put that knowledge of God into action in your life.

What is wisdom according to God? Wisdom is knowing the greatest goal in any situation, and the best way to achieve that goal. Wisdom is different from knowledge because you can have knowledge without wisdom.

There are some brilliant minds in this world. I mean they have the ability to go further than my mind can, but when it comes to faith, they will explain away God and creation with science and theory. How do you accept evolution over creation? Evolution does not make sense.

To discern the best way to achieve a goal, you have to be able to integrate, to fuse all kinds of factors from various sources of knowledge and experience. How can you do that if you will not draw from the true knowledge of the truth from the Word of God?

WISDOM COMES FROM ACTING UPON GOD'S WORD

Wisdom begins by opening the Word of God. If you do not have the knowledge of God, how can you apply it, and if you do not know what God is expecting of us how can we obey it?

James 3:13 says, "Who among you is wise and understanding? Let him show by his good behavior his deeds in the gentleness of wisdom." How do we show the wisdom of God in our life? Through our actions, speech, and how we conduct our lives.

The first part of understanding wisdom is by asking the question, is it from God or the world? He who thinks well, or he who talks well, is not wise in the sense of the Scripture if he does not live and act well.

Look at all the people in this world who have done wrong things by using worldly wisdom. Such wisdom does not come down from above, but springs up from earthly principles, acts on earthly motives, and is intent on serving earthly purposes.

What do the following have in common, jealousy, selfish ambition, and arrogance? All of these traits serve only you. They are all about what satisfies us. What does it profit a man who gains what he cannot keep?

> Mark 8:35-36 "For whoever wishes to save his life will lose it, but whoever loses his life for My sake and the gospel's will save it. 36"For what does it profit a man to gain the whole world, and forfeit his soul?"

Anyone who shows bitter envy and a self-seeking life should not deceive anyone about how "wise" they are. Their "wisdom" is more characteristic of the world, the flesh, and the devil than of God. But for those that have Jesus Christ in their life, we should have the purity, peace, gentleness, teachable spirit, and mercy shown in all our actions. These fruits of righteousness abounding in our lives prove that God has bestowed upon us this excellent gift of wisdom.

The Genuineness of Faith is Based on the Wisdom of God

Paul writes his first letter to the Corinthians to warn the believers against basing their faith on the wisdom of men instead of God's power.

> 1 Corinthians 2:1-7 "And when I came to you, brethren, I did not come with superiority of speech or of wisdom, proclaiming to you the testimony of God. 2 For I determined to know nothing among you except Jesus Christ, and Him crucified. 3 I was with you in weakness and in fear and in much trembling, 4 and my message and my preaching were not in persuasive words of wisdom, but in demonstration of the Spirit and of power, 5 so that your faith would not rest on the wisdom of men, but on the power of God. 6 Yet we do speak wisdom among those who are mature; a wisdom, however, not of this age nor of the rulers of this age, who are passing away; 7 but we speak God's wisdom in a mystery, the hidden wisdom which God predestined before the ages to our glory;"

If you try to base saving faith on the "wisdom of men" it ceases to be saving faith. The content of true faith, which is salvation that comes from Jesus Christ alone, is regarded as foolishness by the world's wisdom.

What is the difference between God's Wisdom and man's wisdom? Wisdom of the world is the use of the human mind to achieve and maintain a ground for boasting before God and man. God's wisdom is taking from the creator all the knowledge that we have been given and applying it to our lives to achieve God's glory.

Why is it so crucial for our faith not to rest in the wisdom of men but in the power of God? Because if it rests in the wisdom of men, it is a bogus faith. So how can I hope to purify my behavior when it flows from my corrupt inward character?

Wisdom understands the impossibility of living the Christian life, for example, controlling our tongues, by our resources, and then about a spirituality that comes from God. Wisdom is from God and it is attained by reliance on God and knowing His Word. How do we demonstrate the wisdom of God?

> 2 Peter 1:2-3 "Grace and peace be multiplied to you in the knowledge of God and of Jesus our Lord; 3seeing that His divine power has granted to us everything pertaining to life and godliness, through the true knowledge of Him who called us by His glory and excellence."

First, we understand that God has given us what we need in the knowledge of Him and everything about life and godliness. Since we have been given the knowledge, it is a matter of applying the knowledge in wisdom to use God's Word as we live our lives.

James 3:17-18 "But the wisdom from above is first pure, then peaceable, gentle, reasonable, full of mercy and good fruits, unwavering, without hypocrisy. 18 And the seed whose fruit is righteousness is sown in peace by those who make peace."

Applying the Knowledge of Jesus Christ to Our Life

To apply the knowledge and wisdom of God we must first trust in God's wisdom for living, rather than trusting in our own knowledge. The second is living in the wisdom of God to carry out his work in our life. What good is it if we have the knowledge yet never use it?

Do you remember when you had to take tests in high school? The teachers would give us tests on the information we had learned. That is how the teachers knew we learned something. Now the question is what did we do with the information after we had it shoved into our brains? If you were like me, every summer would roll around and we would most likely forget what we had learned. Is it the same for your Christian life? Do we hear it and then let it slip away from our minds, or do we continue to learn and grow from the knowledge of God's Word daily?

How do we handle the truth of God's Word? Do we use the wisdom of God for the glory of God? Psalm 1:1 says, "We meditate on it day and night" We use it to live a Godly life and the result is a life of worship to God.

2 Peter 1:5-9 "Now for this very reason also, applying all diligence, in your faith supply moral excellence, and in your moral excellence, knowledge, 6and in your knowledge, self-control, and in your self-control, perseverance, and in your perseverance, godliness, 7and in your godliness, brotherly kindness, and in your brotherly kindness, love. 8For if these qualities are yours and are increasing, they render you neither useless nor unfruitful in the true knowledge of our Lord Jesus Christ. 9For he who lacks these qualities is blind or short-sighted, having forgotten his purification from his former sins."

The wisdom of God is not to be heard and thrown aside, yet applied, and used to help you grow stronger in your relationship with Jesus Christ. The result of this growth in the relationship is a life that is lived as an example of what God can do through you.

"The wisdom of God tells us that God will bring about the best possible results, by the best possible means, for the most possible people, for the longest possible time." (Charles Ryrie, "As He Longs for You to See Him", p. 128.)

Knowledge is the information you have learned; wisdom is the action of taking what you learned and applying it to your life. How will you live in a way that gives glory to God? How will you use God's Word to not only impact your life but impacts those around you when you are called to love?

9

THE MOTIVATION TO LIVE A GODLY LIFE

HOW MANY OF US HAVE BEEN TOLD BY OUR FATHERS OR grandfathers, "Measure twice, cut once"? The reason you measure twice is to double-check your measurements for accuracy before cutting a piece of wood; otherwise, it may be necessary to cut again, wasting time, materials, and money. The "measure twice, cut once" principle can be applied to many facets of life and to more significant decisions than where to saw a piece of wood. Maybe we have measured life a hundred different ways and with each of those cuts, discovered that what we put our faith in came up short and left us unfulfilled. That we have wasted too much time and energy stubbornly trying to force something to fit in our life that wouldn't. Just as there is a correct measurement in building something, there is a correct answer with God's word. The problem is when people decide to start cutting without making sure they are doing what is right with God.

We live in a world where we are taught to plan ahead. In the financial aspect of our life, we scrimp and save for the future by investing in retirement plans so that when we are older, we will not have to worry about how we are going to pay the bills.

In the area of our health, we exercise, (or at least think about exercising) and we try to eat right (or at least don't eat that whole box of Twinkies at one time). We seek advice about our health from sources that range from Woman's Day magazine to an actual doctor who has a degree. But what about the actions of how we live? So, in the matter of how we live, what does it look like? In the last chapter we discovered the wisdom of living a Godly life, now let us look at the motivation behind it.

Who Has Priority in Your Life?

Where are the priorities in your life? Family, friends, money, or living the way we want with the pleasures of this world? So much of our lives is about living for something. What about you? What do you live for?

Do you covet what your neighbors have? Are you striving to be wealthy? Are you trying to be famous? Are you trying to get all you can out of life for your benefit? When we try to do these types of things, we let our focus become so distorted. Because we focus on everything else around us and we miss out on what it means to really live in Christ. We are not called to just live for today, we are called to live for eternity.

How much of your life have you put yourself first above others? How much of your life have you put yourself before God? The truth is that all of us have done this at some point in our life, we have been unfaithful to God.

When we think of our relationship with God, we need to think of it as a marriage commitment. Do you let the things of this world take priority above our love for Christ?

James 4:3-4 "You ask and do not receive, because you ask with wrong motives, so that you may spend it on your pleasures. 4 You adulteresses, do you not know that friendship with the world is hostility toward God?"

The unfaithful behavior that James speaks about has those who have placed their relationship with God in such jeopardy that they are called adulterers and adulteresses. Friendship with the world destroys a person's fellowship with God. Even in our relationship with God, we try to find what will fulfill our life with the pleasures of our sin and pride rather than seeking God to fulfill our life with what we need. Here is the question we must all ask ourselves, what motivates you?

I am a treasure hunter. I love the thrill of the hunt. I have gone on trips to scuba dive on sunken ships that were lost years ago, just to uncover the treasures that they held. I have stood in a cold creek knee-deep in water panning for those speckles of gold. I have followed maps and riddles just trying to discover the path that was taken. I have often dreamed about going on a quest to find a treasure. Why would I do that? I am an explorer. I kind of think of myself as the Indiana Jones type of guy who is always looking for the chance to take an adventure. I want the thrill of the chase and the adventure of the journey in the hunt for the treasures

What are the wrong motives for asking for something from God? Is it wrong to be a treasure hunter? No. Is it wrong to want the adventure? No, but what about if it goes against God's Word, God's character, and God's designed purpose for your life? Then yes.

We spend so much of our life fitting into the mold of being human beings. Fitting into the norm of society, but as Christians, we are called to a higher standard. We are called to represent Jesus Christ to this world. But so much of our lives have become about living for me and what I can achieve. Where does God fall into that picture of your life?

We imagine that life is this grand event of being fulfilled with the things that make us happy. What about God, what makes God happy? Does he enjoy watching you enjoy a sunrise or a sunset? Does God not enjoy it when you jump into a pool of water on a hot summer's day? Does God not enjoy when you smell the beautiful flowers of His creation? Think of this, He created these things with you in mind. God didn't have to make this beautiful world full of seasons and glorious depictions of His majesty, he didn't have to make things so beautiful and diverse, he didn't have to make the things, we take for granted every day, like family and friendships, nature, taste, and smells, but he did and He did it for us.

Why did God create humans? It wasn't that he was lonely. He did so to give himself glory. God created us to live and enjoy a relationship with him. Jesus said, "I have told you this so that my joy may be in you and that your joy may be complete" (John 15:11). Because of his great love, because of who he is, he gave us all the wonderful gifts of this world and in our lives because he loves us.

I think we often think about how short life is. David tells us in Psalm 144:4 "Man is like a mere breath; His days are like a passing shadow."

Psalm 90:12-14 "So teach us to number our days, That we may present to You a heart of wisdom. 13 Do return, O Lord; how long will it be? And be sorry for Your servants. 14 O satisfy us in the morning with Your lovingkindness, That we may sing for joy and be glad all our days."

We spend so much of the time of our life trying to make ourselves happy, that we miss out on the true commitment of God and how he has called us to live.

THE PRIORITY OF LIVING A GODLY LIFE

The direction of our life is not about ourselves, but for Christ. What are the two greatest commandments? Love God and love others. God did not say, God first and you second. He said, love others second.

Matthew 22:37-40 "You shall love the Lord God with all your heart, and with all your soul, and with all your mind.' 38"This is the great and foremost commandment. 39"The second is like it, 'you shall love your neighbor as yourself.' 40"On these two commandments depend the whole Law and the Prophets."

What would happen if we lived for others before ourselves? Do you think we would live in the same world we live in today? What if we gave to help others more? Would people go hungry? What if we gave more of our time? Would we need fewer mental hospitals or jails? What if we decided to love not based on beauty, but the need for love? What difference would that make in the world? The sad reality is that we don't love as we should.

We live in a world of greed, selfishness, anger, hatred, and the love of self. Where has that gotten us? We have built a deprived, hurtful, vengeful nation driven on the idea of "Me first". What is disheartening is that it has even flowed over into the churches. When you hear people say; "Pastor, preach what makes me happy", "Pastor, tell me I'm the most important", "Pastor, tell me that the world revolves around me."

Scripture has been replaced by the "what I think" and "How I feel" attitudes. It is no longer what God says, but more what I think, how I feel, and what I want. What has become of the Word of God in churches today, is the Word of God just another good book to read on the lineup of best sellers?

The Bible is the only book by which we live, teach, and receive instructions when it comes to living our lives for God. People no longer want to hear what God says, they want to hear what they want.

> James 4:4-5 "You adulteresses, do you not know that friendship with the world is hostility toward God? Therefore whoever wishes to be a friend of the world makes himself an enemy of God. 5 Or do you think that the Scripture speaks to no purpose: "He jealously desires the Spirit which He has made to dwell in us"?

This is a rebuke in Old Testament vocabulary. God spoke this way in the Old Testament when His people were attracted to some form of idolatry (Jeremiah 3:8-9, Ezekiel 6:9, Ezekiel 16:32,

Ezekiel 23:37, and Hosea 3:1). Their covetousness is idolatry (Colossians 3:5) and friendship with the world.

ANYTHING THAT COMES BEFORE GOD CAN BECOME AN IDOL

We cannot both be friends of this world system in rebellion against God, and friends of God at the same time (Matthew 6:24). Even the desire to be a friend of the world makes one an enemy of God.

Have you seen the bumper stickers on cars that read, "COEXIST"? This is what the world says, accept every religion, and every god. This is not what God says, God says friends with the world are enemies against God. The assertion that all faiths are the same and there is no exclusive truth is itself a doctrine and one that excludes all but the Universalist. It represents an incoherent quest for tolerance. The real danger of the Coexist movement is its underlying assumption that how we live is ultimately a matter of human agency. Coexistence treats Jesus Christ merely as an important moral teacher and disregards that he revealed himself as God.

If we are a believer in Jesus Christ then the indwelling presence of the Holy Spirit has a jealous yearning for our friendship with God. The Christian who lives in compromise cannot help but be convicted by it. How long will we keep denying the voice of the Holy Spirit in our lives? How long will we choose to deny God as the priority in our life?

How could God love someone who thinks of themselves first in sin, in finances, and in living for ourselves versus living for God? How I want it to be, the way I want my life, and how I decide to live my life. The answer is simple. God's love goes beyond my sin.

Worldliness is a problem in the church. A worldly Christian

tries to love Jesus and the world at the same time. They are trying to serve two masters at the same time. The worldly Christian wants Jesus to give him lots of money to buy a lot of stuff and power so that he can enjoy the pleasures of this world. He refuses to love God wholeheartedly. Such a person may read the Bible and go to church, but soon the worries of this temporal life, the deceitfulness of wealth, and the pleasures of this earthly life choke and kill his interest in the gospel.

God's Grace and His Motivation

We have been given the Holy Spirit. The Holy Spirit not only instructs us, but he also empowers us and pours out God's love in abundance into our hearts, that we may love God and one another. The Holy Spirit has one other important role, and that is to give believers wisdom by which we can understand God.

> 1 Corinthians 2:9-12 "What no eye has seen, what no ear has heard, and what no human mind has conceived" the things God has prepared for those who love him 10 these are the things God has revealed to us by his Spirit. The Spirit searches all things, even the deep things of God. 11 For who knows a person's thoughts except their own spirit within them? In the same way no one knows the thoughts of God except the Spirit of God. 12 What we have received is not the spirit of the world, but the Spirit who is from God, so that we may understand what God has freely given us."

Leo Tolstoy was a Russian writer who is regarded as one of the greatest authors of all time, also had a profound love for Christ. He wrote this concerning his life:

"Love is life. All, everything that I understand, I understand only because I love. Everything is, everything exists, only because I love. Everything is united by it alone. Love is God, and to die means that I, a particle of love, shall return to the general and eternal source." (Leo Tolstoy: War and Peace Book Twelve 1812 16. CHAPTER XVI)

Is your life a living example of the love of God? Living a holy life for God in a hostile world is hard, for the world hates us as it hated our Lord Jesus Christ.

God actively and continually opposes the proud, the idolaters, the worldly people, the devil worshipers, but God also continually gives greater grace to humble believers so that they may live in this present evil age in a way that is pleasing to God.

> Philippians 2:12-13 "So then, my beloved, just as you have always obeyed, not as in my presence only, but now much more in my absence, work out your salvation with fear and trembling; 13 for it is God who is at work in you, both to will and to work for His good pleasure."

God not only grants us the power to live for him but the desire to do so as we are led to live a committed life for Jesus Christ. It is through his love and divine attributes are given to us through the Holy Spirit that we commit our ways to love him more, by putting him at the center focus of our life.

Jesus is looking for followers that are passionately following him. He does not want you to follow him on your terms, he wants us to be fully devoted to him one hundred percent.

The most challenging part of living for Christ is knowing, and maturing in the person of Christ daily. Following Jesus doesn't work unless we die to ourselves every day. Not only are Christians born again when we come to salvation, but we also continue dying to self as part of the process of sanctification. As such, dying to self is both a one-time event and a lifelong process.

> Matthew 16:24-25 "Then Jesus said to his disciples, "Whoever wants to be my disciple must deny themselves and take up their cross and follow me. 25 For whoever wants to save their life will lose it, but whoever loses their life for me will find it."

10

THE PURPOSE OF LIVING THE GODLY LIFE

A FELLOW WAS ON TOP OF THE ROOF OF HIS SECOND-STORY HOME putting up a television antenna. It was large and tall, and he was trying to attach the guide wires from the antenna to a section of the roof. The wind was blowing making it even more difficult. Suddenly he began to slip, and he slid down the roof until he caught himself on the little metal rain gutter that went around the eves of the second floor. In a panic, he held on and screamed up to heaven, "Isn't there anybody up there who can help me?" And a voice from heaven came, "I can help you." "Well, what shall I do?" "Let go and I will catch you." The man then yells out, "Is there anybody else up there who can help me?"

In all of our lives, we have a point that we must submit to someone. Whether it's a boss, a parent, or someone who is in charge because of years of experience, there is a point in our life where we must give control. How do we determine who we decide to give control to? Because that is what it comes down to is submission. Submission is when we remove our pride and allow someone else to take control.

When an officer pulls you over, do you decide to stop your car or keep going? When you pull over, you are submitting to his authority granted by the state. When you are asked to do something, do you do it or do you refuse to do what has been asked of you? The same question can be asked in our Christian lives.

Sometimes it seems like it is a struggle of me versus God. We don't like to think of it this way, but it's true. Answer this question, who is more important in my life, me or God? Of course, we would want to answer God, but does that show in our life?

How can we have a perfect relationship and communication with God? It begins by submitting to God in our minds and our attitude. We must determine if we will stand as a proud person telling God what we will do, or telling God what he must do in our relationship. Do we trust God knows what is best for our life? Following his direction, for his purpose, or do we do what we think is best? This is where we find most of the struggles we face with God. He created us to live in harmony with him and to enjoy life. He created us with the desire for relationships, but so many unfortunately chose to live separate from God in the hope of living a good life on their own.

MAKING THE DECISION TO FOLLOW GOD'S DIRECTION

Which would you rather have; the resistance from God or grace from God? Well, that's simple you would say, "I want greater grace". You have to understand humility brings grace; pride brings resistance. But how do you get that humility?

When you go to an interview, you never tell whoever is interviewing you, "I know it all, I don't need your help. Just hire me because I am the best." How well do you think that would go over? James 4:7 says "Therefore submit to God. Resist the devil and he will flee from you."

In all the New Testament incidents where the word submit occurs, the word is translated from the Greek word hupotasso, (Hoopo -tas'-so). The hupo means "under" and the tasso means "to arrange." In essence, "to arrange who has priority in your life."

> James 4:7-8 "Submit therefore to God. Resist the devil and he will flee from you. 8 Draw near to God and He will draw near to you. Cleanse your hands, you sinners; and purify your hearts, you double-minded."

How do we receive Grace? Submit to God. You cannot have grace until you submit to God. You cannot resist the devil until you submit to God. What does submission look like? It begins by first deciding to accept the free gift of salvation through Jesus Christ. Without this first point, there can be no change. Then once we have a relationship with Jesus Christ, we need to make a daily choice to submit ourselves to God for the work that the Holy Spirit does in us to "conform us to the image of Christ." Notice that keyword, daily.

MAKING YOURSELF AVAILABLE TO GOD

Imagine you were to only eat once a week on a Sunday? What if you only ate every other day, would it impact your life? Of course. The truth is that it is the same with God's Word in our life. Because there are so many things in this world trying to take our attention, trying to pull us away from God, attracting us to say in our hearts "Me first". This is why we need that daily choice to say, "God, I want you to be in my actions, my words and I want my life to represent you".

We can even equate submission to the idea of a bondservant. A bondservant gives himself up to another's will, those whose service is used by Christ in extending and advancing His cause among men.

In many New Testament books, the word bondservant was used about a person's commitment to Jesus. Most of Paul's letters begin by referring to himself as a servant of Christ Jesus. James and Jude, half-brothers of Jesus, both refer to themselves as Christ's bondservants. The apostle Peter called himself a "servant and apostle" (2 Peter 1:1).

Despite proclaiming a message of freedom from sin in Jesus Christ, these writers were dedicated to Jesus as their one master. A bondservant was more than an employee who could leave for another job, these Christians were servants who would never leave their master for another.

As a bondservant, we make ourselves available to God. Each day we must choose to submit to God for the process of learning to grow spiritually. It is a process that began with salvation and is ongoing with every choice that we make to submit ourselves to God. It doesn't end after a couple of years. This process will continue until the Lord comes again or he calls us home.

In the Old Testament, we read in Exodus where if a master has a slave and at the end of his term or endured service is done with the master, if the slave chooses to stay with his master because of the love he has for the master and chooses to stay in service, then the master is to take the servant first to God, then he shall bring him to the door or the doorpost in the city square and his master shall pierce his ear with an awl; and he shall serve him permanently. (Exodus 21:5) Not because he has to, but because he wanted to.

For us, as Christians, our ears have not been pierced, but something more valuable to us, it has been our heart that was pierced. When we said yes to Jesus, our whole lives were changed. At that moment we said, "Jesus, I am completely your", Jesus took control and the Holy Spirit came into our lives and we started that relationship that would make us a whole new person. By accepting Jesus, we have dedicated our lives to serving him. 1 Corinthians 6:20 says, "For you have been bought with a price: therefore, glorify God in your body."

God does not say serve me or else. God does not want a slave, God wants us to love him, and because we love him, we have the desire to follow Him, and we want to dedicate our lives to glorify him.

LIVING A LIFE OF OBEDIENCE TO GOD

The idea of the relationship we have with God is not a master and slave, but Father to his child.

The first part of living an obedient life is to humble ourselves. What is the result of humbling ourselves before God? It is the free gift of salvation offered through Jesus Christ.

> 2 Timothy 2:11 "It is a trustworthy statement: For if we died with Him, we will also live with Him; 12If we endure, we will also reign with Him; If we deny Him, He also will deny us; 13If we are faithless, He remains faithful, for He cannot deny Himself."

> Ephesians 2:10 "For we are His workmanship created in Christ Jesus for good works, which God prepared beforehand that we should walk in them."

By humbling ourselves before God, he uses us for his purpose. We can live a life that is glorifying to God.

One day as we stand before the throne of God there will be one who will look at the things we have done in life and judge them according to our actions. Now don't get me wrong, for those of us who are Christians we will stand before the throne of God at the Bema seat, not to be judged before God for our sins, because all of our sins are washed away. God says he remembers our sins no more. When we stand before God it will be our reward ceremony.

> James 4:13-17 "Come now, you who say, "Today or tomorrow we will go to such and such a city, and spend a year there and engage in business and make a profit." 14 Yet you do not know what your life will be like tomorrow. You are just a vapor that appears for a little while and then vanishes away. 15 Instead, you ought to say, "If the Lord wills, we will live and also do this or that." 16 But as it is, you boast in your arrogance; all such boasting is evil. 17 Therefore, to one who knows the right thing to do and does not do it, to him it is sin.

TRUSTING IN GOD'S PLAN FOR OUR LIFE

With this in mind, how is Christ calling us to live? With God as the focus of our life. If life is but a vapor it means, life is short. How will we live with the time that we have? We do not know how long we will be allowed to remain here on earth, but as believers, our time and our plans will be better and sweeter if we trust him with the plans of our life instead of fighting against him.

When we make plans and decisions, we must believe that God knows what is best. We must know that God is in control of what is best for our lives. As Christians, do we believe God knows what He is doing? Do we trust that He is in control even when we don't understand how or why? Do we trust Him in the big stuff and the little stuff? And do we believe that he has a plan for our lives and that his plans are perfect?

This life that we live, the very breath in our bodies is a daily gift from God. We will be accountable for everything God has given us and what we have done with them for his glory. At the end of our life God is going to look at our life and not condemn us for our actions, but hold us accountable for what has been entrusted to us, his church, his Word, and his message of Salvation and the Gift of Jesus Christ.

Understand that we are called to live a life for Jesus and resist living in sin and strive to live a life Holy and pleasing to God.

> Romans 12:1-2 "1Therefore I urge you, brethren, by the mercies of God, to present your bodies a living and holy sacrifice, acceptable to God, which is your spiritual service of worship. 2And do not be conformed to this world, but be transformed by the renewing of your mind, so that you may prove what the will of God is, that which is good and acceptable and perfect."

God has delivered from the penalties of your sin and now he is calling each one of us to live a life, resisting the devil and submitting to him. God created us and loves us and he wants to do something amazing with your life if you let Him.

We are not promised tomorrow so how will you live your life, for yourself or God? Will you live the life that says Jesus is my King? Will you have a heart of obedience or one of pride? And today will you decide to draw closer to God in your relationship with Him?

I do not know the future, but I do know who holds the future and I don't know what he has for you and me, but we can be confident in this, that what God has in store for us is way better than what you or I deserve.

11

USING WHAT GOD HAS GIVEN YOU

You may find that most pastors do not preach a lot on stewardship. It's easy to understand, but why do we tiptoe around the subject? Because money is still a god to many people and some may be skeptical of the church's motives with their tithes.

Even though preaching on money turns some people off, some are turned off when we preach on forgiveness, too. But we don't apologize. We say what God's Word says and let it have the final results in a person's life. I have come to realize that we may not be mature disciples if we have not embraced the reality that materially we are stewards instead of owners.

> James 5:1- 3 "Come now, you rich people, weep and howl for your miseries which are coming upon you. 2 Your riches have rotted and your garments have become moth-eaten. 3 Your gold and your silver have corroded, and their corrosion will serve as a testimony against you and will consume your flesh like fire. It is in the last days that you have stored up your treasure!"

The trouble for many believers is that they live a divided life. Just as we are both guilty and declared righteous at the same time.

We are sinners, bought with the blood of Christ and so righteous because of Jesus, yet still guilty of the sins that we do. We are children of two worlds: heaven and earth.

We walk through life indulging in every earthly pleasure while realizing that the truth is it's only the beginning for us. We have eternity to taste of God's goodness, and every pleasure and blessing we have ever heard of was ultimately orchestrated by His good hand.

In this world, there is a mindset that one of the priorities in life is to be rich. This is how people think that they have had a good life, don't believe me? Take a look at power-ball, the lottery, casinos, scratch-off tickets, the list can go on and on. With money, all of us would love to attain it, but most of us don't believe we have enough of it.

WE ARE GOD'S STEWARDS

When it comes to wealth, the Bible and the world have very different concepts of what wealth is. The world's definition of wealth is an abundance of valuable material possessions or resources. Each one of us puts a very different realm on what wealth is to us.

Grandparents will say, "it is the grandchildren in their life that brings them wealth". Another may say "they always thought of wealth as being "rich", and having the fancy car and the huge house.

Wealth involves many things, including money, happiness, time, health, attitude, relationships, lifestyle, peace of mind, and any other thing you desire for what you view as a successful life. If you have a family like our church, you may be considered wealthy to someone else who has no church or has no family. Even for many people, the idea of wealth is to make as much now, work as hard as you can, to get as much as you can, to be rich at the end of your life when you're too old to spend it.

In light of our short unknown time on this earth, do we share what God has given us to make a difference on His behalf? All we have is attributed to what God has given us. God wants us to realize the great responsibility of his riches that he has entrusted to us, to use us for his glory, and to be part of his plan.

Think back on the wonderful things God has done in our lives. As believers, we need to wake ourselves up to the great responsibility that comes to us because so much has been given to us. Many see the responsibility of giving as a burden. How sad that is in light of Paul's reminder that God loves a cheerful giver, that some consider what God has given them a burden. Giving is a relational decision. In the process of making decisions about giving, we establish our agreement with God about stewardship. As God's stewards, our decisions on giving are simply a matter of thinking through how he wants us to allocate his money.

An amazing benefit of giving as stewards is that it releases us from the real burden of our own financial needs. As we learn to trust God through giving, we can live confidently on what is left because we know that God is taking care of our needs. The outcome for those who give as stewards is that they experience a sense of intimacy with God that all followers of Christ long for. When we give it becomes an act of worship. Giving becomes a way of saying thanks to God for his grace and promised provision, it becomes a deep part of our connection to God.

Have you ever had a time in your life when God told you to give money to someone? God has done this in our life so many times. When God told us of a need and laid it upon our hearts to give, we followed through with what God was asking us to do. The amazing thing was, that both myself and my wife knew that it was God speaking to us at different times. When I brought up giving, she said she felt God saying the same thing. This was no coincidence. There was that connection to God as he laid it upon both of our hearts to give. The Lord speaks directly through us by the Holy Spirit.

The amazing thing about God working in us is that He uses our lives to touch other people's lives. There is a saying that says, "With great power comes great responsibility". This also applies to being a steward for God. God's riches bring great responsibility to act on his behalf.

Jesus said in Luke 12:48, "Everyone to whom much is given, from him much will be required." It is so easy for money to come and go. Most things of this world won't last beyond this world, and believers should recognize that.

Think about this, if I buy that red Ferrari, I tie up the resources on personal pleasures that God gave me to reach others and eternally change destinies. That is four hundred and twenty-five thousand dollars for a car, ($425,000). I am just thankful for a car that runs rather than a status symbol. We need to ask the question, "Do my pleasures take the place of honoring God with my finances?"

Now do not get me wrong, earthly treasures are not wrong to own, they are just temporary. The things we place value in can be considered "Our treasures"

WE ONLY HAVE WHAT GOD HAS GIVEN US

When it comes to our finances, how are we investing what God has entrusted to us in the kingdom of God and how are we supporting the ministries of God that he has called us to give?

We strive to put away so much to be set for the future, but what about the future in heaven? Are Christians more concerned about gaining acceptance in the world and appealing to the world gaining our earthly treasures or what about what God is doing now?

> Matthew 6:19-21 "Do not store up for yourselves treasures on earth, where moth and rust destroy, and where thieves break in and steal. 20"But store up for yourselves treasures in heaven, where neither moth nor rust destroys, and where thieves do not break in or steal; 21for where your treasure is, there your heart will be also."

When God is the owner of our finances and we are mere stewards, perhaps it's time to be reminded of what God is doing through you. Psalm 24: 1 says, "The earth is the Lord's, and all it contains, the world, and those who dwell in it."

Our riches are not in the things we have, but in how we can impact other people with what God has given us. Are we magnifying Jesus in our giving? The main principle behind tithing and giving is the fact that what we do with our money shows where our heart is. Matthew 6:21 says "For where your treasure is, there your heart will be also." When we can give ten percent or more of our income, instead of keeping that money for ourselves, it shows that our heart isn't tied to our money and that we love God more than our money.

The Bible mentions money over eight hundred times and of all of Jesus' parables, more than half of them talked about money. Why? Because that is where so many people get tripped up. We must remember that everything we have has been given to us by Him.

> Malachi 3:10 "Bring the whole tithe into the storehouse, so that there may be food in My house, and test Me now in this," says the LORD of hosts, "if I will not open for you the windows of heaven and pour out for you a blessing until it overflows"

GIVING TEACHES CONTENTMENT

2 Timothy 2:13 says, "If we are faithless, He remains faithful, for He cannot deny Himself." God says for us to prove him faithful. Why is it so hard to do? Because there is the mentality that "if I give it, I won't have it". God who is always faithful says, "Try Me". He will always prove himself true to his word because he can do no less. Does God need your money? No. Here is where we miss out, God chooses to use us to make the impact. God makes us partners in his ministry through giving. God chooses you to make a difference in a community, he chooses you to reach others around the world through missionaries, he chooses you to impact others through your local church.

God can do it on his own, but he is growing you, allowing you to minister to others around us. Some people in the church miss out on the blessings of God by not following God's challenge to see God's faithfulness. They fail to have the joy of giving to the Lord, they fail to receive the blessing of being a cheerful giver. I want you to see what God has said about giving and living in the blessings of His abundance in 2 Corinthians 9:6.

> 2 Corinthians 9:6-8 "Now this I say, he who sows sparingly will also reap sparingly, and he who sows bountifully will also reap bountifully. 7Each one must do just as he has purposed in his heart, not grudgingly or under compulsion, for God loves a cheerful giver. 8And God is able to make all grace abound to you, so that always having all sufficiency in everything, you may have an abundance for every good deed;"

> 2 Corinthians 9:12-15 "For the ministry of this service is not only fully supplying the needs of the saints but is also overflowing through many thanksgivings to God. 13Because of the proof given by this ministry, they will glorify God for your obedience to your confession of the gospel of Christ and the liberality of your contribution to them and to all, 14while they also, by prayer on your behalf, yearn for you because of the surpassing grace of God in you. 15Thanks be to God for His indescribable gift!"

GIVING GROWS OUR FAITH IN GOD

The bible talks about giving as an indescribable gift. First, we need to understand God owns everything. We are simply managers or administrators acting on his behalf. Therefore, stewardship expresses our obedience regarding the administration of everything God has placed under our control, which is all-encompassing.

Stewardship is the commitment of one's self and possessions to God's service, recognizing that we do not have the right of control over our property or ourselves. When we give it connects us with God personally. That's where the worship of giving happens. It costs.

King David once said I will not sacrifice a burnt offering that costs me nothing (1 Chronicle 21:24).

> Colossians 3:23-24 "Whatever you do, do your work heartily, as for the Lord rather than for men, 24 knowing that from the Lord you will receive the reward of the inheritance. It is the Lord Christ whom you serve."

The people in the prophet Malachi's day had treated God badly by robbing him. They had become bored with God. Their worship had turned from relational to ritual. As a result, they offered blemished sacrifices (1:6-14); the priests had become unfaithful (2:1-9); divorce was commonplace and easy (2:10-17); their words wearied God (2:17); businessmen were defrauding their workers, cheating their customers, and taking advantage of widows, orphans, and aliens (3:1-5). But the most egregious treatment of God was that they were robbing God (3:6-12).

How could someone rob God? By withholding their tithes, by giving the worst instead of the best, by giving the least and not the most.

> Malachi 3:8 "Will a man rob God? Yet you are robbing Me! But you say, 'How have we robbed You?' In tithes and offerings. 9 You are cursed with a curse, for you are robbing Me, the whole nation of you! 10 Bring the whole tithe into the storehouse, so that there may be food in My house, and test Me now in this," says the Lord of hosts, "if I will not open for you the windows of heaven and pour out for you a blessing until it overflows. 11 Then I will rebuke the devourer for you so that it will not destroy the fruits of the ground; nor will your vine in the field cast its grapes," says the Lord of hosts. 12 "All the nations will call you blessed, for you shall be a delightful land," says the Lord of hosts."

God expects that what he has given us is to be used to make a difference to those around us with the expectation of bringing glory to God. God calls each of us to glorify him in all we do. One of the ways God glorifies himself is by calling and enabling us to glorify him through our holy conduct.

> Luke 12:48b "...From everyone who has been given much, much will be demanded; and to whom they entrusted much, of him they will ask all the more."

> 1 Corinthians 10:31 "Therefore, whether you eat or drink, or whatever you do, do all things for the glory of God."

GIVING IS WORSHIP

The computer program, Google Earth, allows you to zoom down from a picture of the globe to the level of your house through satellite photos. When I zoom down to a picture of our church property, I can see my car parked out front on the day the satellite took the picture. When I zoomed down to my house, I could even see my grill on the patio. But what strikes me as the computer is zooming down is how very tiny my home is in the perspective of the earth. Even if I owned ten square miles of land and houses, or owned the Taj Mahal, I would still own very little. But God owns the whole earth (Ps. 24:1)

Our giving and our support to ministry are big in God's grand scheme only if the gift acknowledges and worships the real giver, and the real owner. Giving is worship. Proverbs 3:9 says, "Honor the LORD with your wealth, with the first fruits of all your crops."

Ask yourself this question, are you honoring God with your giving? Not only with your money, but your time, your gifts, and your talent. Are you investing this day in the Kingdom of God or your earthly desires? Are you storing up treasures in heaven or on earth?

12

COMMITTED TO GOD IN PRAYER

SOME PEOPLE WONDER WHY THEIR PRAYERS ARE NOT ANSWERED. When we pray, how do we usually come to God? Most of the time it seems we come wanting something, "Lord I need, Lord, I want, Lord, if you would only"

For us as believers, prayer is an important part of our life. But most of the time we use prayer as if God is a genie in a bottle. To be honest, isn't it true that we usually go to God in prayer because we want something? "Lord, something is wrong and I can't fix it. Can you?" Oh Lord, why have you brought these pains upon me?" "Dear Lord, you know of that problem I have. Can you get me out of it?" Time after time we come to God, in a "woe is me state". But how often have we come to God because what has come upon us is caused by our faults?

GOD'S WORD CALLS US TO PRAY WITHOUT CEASING.

> 1 Thessalonians 5:16-18 says, "Rejoice always, 17 pray without ceasing, 18 in everything give thanks; for this is the will of God for you in Christ Jesus.

> James 5:13"Is anyone cheerful? He is to sing praises."

What is the difference between prayer and praise? Prayer is coming to God to talk to him, but much of the time, it is us coming to get something. We take this prayer out of context. Yes, God wants us to come to him with our needs, but why? Doesn't he know what we need? Yes, God knows our needs, but it is the part where we communicate with God on a personal basis. Prayer is the only way to a real and personal relationship with God.

First of all, prayer acknowledges He is God, and that you accept His gracious gift, Jesus Christ, as your Lord and Savior (Genesis 17:1, Romans 6:16-18). Prayer is our part of confessing our sins and accepting His forgiveness (Romans 3:23-26). Prayer is also that part of our lives that asks for his will in us. That His Holy Spirit would guide us, and that we be filled with the fullness of all God has for us. We pray for understanding and wisdom (Proverbs 2:6-8, Proverbs 3:5). We pray with thanksgiving for all the ways He blesses us (Philippians 4:6). We pray when we are ill, and going through trials or interceding for others (James 5:14-16, 2 Corinthians 12:9-10). But Prayer is also a way of worshiping Him

> Psalm 95:6-7 "Come, let us worship and bow down, Let us kneel before the Lord our Maker.7 For He is our God, And we are the people of His pasture and the sheep of His hand."

PRAYER IS A KEY TO KNOWING THE HEART OF GOD

Have you realized that there is nothing we cannot pray about and there is nothing that we cannot go to God for? The Bible tells us to "pray without ceasing" and "in everything give thanks to the Lord." When we choose to have a positive attitude, we realize we have received many blessings for which to give God praise. We find intimacy with God through communicating with Him in prayer.

Just as a man and woman in love desire to be together and communicate, so we, if we love God, will desire to be with him and to fellowship with Him in proportion to our love for him.

PRAYER ALLOWS US TO PARTICIPATE IN GOD'S WORK

Isn't it amazing that God chose you and me to be part of his plan when he could do it without us? God chooses to say, "I want you to experience what I experience when I help others and when I show love to others." God thinks of us enough to use us to work in others' lives. To take part in reaching others, to take part in serving the greater purpose of others knowing the love of God.

> Ephesians 2:10 "For we are His workmanship, created in Christ Jesus for good works, which God prepared beforehand so that we would walk in them.

When we go to God by faith, we have the knowledge that he hears and answers all our prayers (1 John 5:14). Prayer grants us the privilege of experiencing God. Be confident that God knows and wants what is best for us; so, ask that his will be done in all we seek from him. Then, thank him for it, even though it hasn't happened yet. What we are doing by going to God in prayer is exercising our confidence and faith in God. There is never a time God does not want us to come to him in prayer. He wants to answer the prayer, yet sometimes we never come to Him.

There are two parts of prayer, first coming to him and praying in obedience and second believing in faith that God is in control. Obedience and faith are simply two parts of one-act as we surrender to God. Faith leads to obedience and obedience strengthens faith. It is a blessed cycle that should characterize Christians.

Think about this, how often do we come to God in prayer seeking him with all our heart? What prayer does is allow us to seek God with all our hearts.

> Jeremiah 29:11-13 "11 "For I know the plans that I have for you,' declares the Lord, 'plans for welfare and not for calamity to give you a future and a hope. 12'Then you will call upon Me and come and pray to Me, and I will listen to you. 13 'You will seek Me and find Me when you search for Me with all your heart. 14'I will be found by you,' declares the Lord".

Prayer should not be done halfheartedly, it must be "with all the heart. Yet we fail to do this. Do we have unwavering confidence in God, a belief that he will do what is best, and a cheerful committing of the cause into his hands?

God answers the prayers in three ways, "Yes, no, and wait a while." "Yes", here is the answer, "No this is not my will for you", and "wait a while" when the perfect time for God's plan or your healing or your restoration will be completed in your life according to his plan and purpose.

THE RESULTS OF PRAYER

James 5:16 "Therefore, confess your sins to one another, and pray for one another so that you may be healed. The effective prayer of a righteous man can accomplish much."

Sometimes praying involves coming to God united with others in prayer. Does it make God listen more? No, of course not. James tells us, "The effective prayer of a righteous man can accomplish much." Or "has great power as it is working." Now, does this mean that only the prayers of good people are heard? No, the word righteous in the Bible refers to those who have faith and are covered by Jesus' righteousness (Romans 5:1; 3:21–22; 4:2–3).

Knowing God and understanding Him is an integral part of prayer. Prayer is not about getting everything we want or keeping others safe, healthy, and problem-free at all times. Prayer is a powerful way in which we get to know our Savior, and it also brings believers together. The effective prayer for others will bring us closer to God because effective prayer is based on a knowledge of his will not mine. 1 John 5:14 "This is the confidence which we have before Him, that, if we ask anything according to His will, He hears us."

Not only by praying for others will it bring us closer to those we pray for, but as we learn more about others' needs, we focus on them and not ourselves.

For most of us, praying for others tends to run along these lines: Lord, provide my friend with a job, a car that runs, good health, and safety. However, most of the prayers recorded in the Bible are of another type.

When Jesus was praying for others, he prayed for their faith (Luke 22:32), he prayed against temptation in their lives (Luke 22:40), he prayed for their unity (John 17:11), and he prayed for their sanctification (John 17:17). Paul prayed that believers would be strengthened by the Spirit, rooted and grounded in love, able to comprehend God's love, and filled with the fullness of God (Ephesians 3:14–19). These are all prayers according to the Father's will.

PRAYER STRENGTHENS THE BONDS BETWEEN BELIEVERS

Praying for others today can help to build up the body of Christ. Are we using prayer to be an impactful servant of the almighty God?

> James 5:17 "Elijah was a man with a nature like ours, and he prayed earnestly that it would not rain, and it did not rain on the earth for three years and six months."

Elijah was like you and me. Just an ordinary person wanting to do the will of the Father. "Elijah prayed earnestly." What does that mean? Elijah prayed with sincere and intense conviction. Does this sound like your prayer life? When you come to God are you sincere with your prayers? Or do you just throw them at

God and say "Here", like throwing papers into the air? Do we pray as if we depend on God? Isn't God our source of life? Isn't he our comfort and strength?

Through prayer, we receive comfort, strength, and all the other resources we need in life, both naturally and spiritually. Prayer is so essential to us, that he commands us to do it all the time.

If you were to examine your prayer life, would it fit the standards on how God has taught us to pray? Would your prayer demonstrate; God is my shepherd, he is my Provider, he is my healer, and he is my peace and my victory?

When we pray in the name of Jesus, it reminds us of who he is and what He has done for you - and that should stir up love in your heart for Him. Prayer is more than just a time of closing your eyes, it is a relational time spent with the God of this Universe who loves you and wants to spend time with you.

CONCLUSION

THE CHRISTIAN LIFE IS NOT JUST US LIVING OUR LIVES FOR JESUS, it is us giving the control of our lives to Jesus so that he can live his life in and through us!

The most important thing in this life is for you and me to remain in our love relationship with Christ, everything else will flow from the abundance of that relationship! What did Jesus say was the most important commandment? To love God.

You cannot simply say that you only have a relationship with Jesus without obedience. If we truly set our focus on developing a healthy active relationship with God, we will naturally start seeing obedience flowing in our lives.

Do you see it yet? It is all about our relationship with Him. Here is the difference between us trying to live for Christ and the Holy Spirit living in us. If we are trying to live our lives for Jesus, that puts the responsibility on us to do all the right things. Living this way will inevitably lead to us feeling like a failure like we aren't good enough. However, when we place our focus simply on relationship with God and allow the "good works" to simply be the natural result of that relationship we find that the responsibility rests on God to produce the fruit in our lives, and in this way, we find freedom and peace.

Man is always trying to find a way to please God when the truth is that God has already made us pleasing to him in Christ. We cannot "maintain our salvation" or our right standing before God. We are already right. Jesus completed the work and we can't add more to it.

131

I truly hope that this helps someone be set free from the bondage that we experience when we believe that we need to do all the right things, and not do all the wrong things. All we are called to do is love God with who we are and allow him to do the work in us.

Printed in the United States
by Baker & Taylor Publisher Services